The Intentional Leader

Dr Donald Davenport

WESTBOW
PRESS®
A DIVISION OF THOMAS NELSON
& ZONDERVAN

Scripture taken from the New King James Version. Copyright © 1979, 1980, 1982 by Thomas Nelson, Inc. Used by permission. All rights reserved.

Scripture taken from the Holy Bible, NEW INTERNATIONAL VERSION®. Copyright © 1973, 1978, 1984 by Biblica, Inc. All rights reserved worldwide. Used by permission. NEW INTERNATIONAL VERSION® and NIV® are registered trademarks of Biblica, Inc. Use of either trademark for the offering of goods or services requires the prior written consent of Biblica US, Inc.

WestBow Press books may be ordered through booksellers or by contacting:

WestBow Press
A Division of Thomas Nelson & Zondervan
1663 Liberty Drive
Bloomington, IN 47403
www.westbowpress.com
1 (866) 928-1240

Because of the dynamic nature of the Internet, any web addresses or links contained in this book may have changed since publication and may no longer be valid. The views expressed in this work are solely those of the author and do not necessarily reflect the views of the publisher, and the publisher hereby disclaims any responsibility for them.

Any people depicted in stock imagery provided by Thinkstock are models, and such images are being used for illustrative purposes only. Certain stock imagery © Thinkstock.

ISBN: 978-1-5127-0862-2 (sc)
ISBN: 978-1-5127-0863-9 (hc)
ISBN: 978-1-5127-0861-5 (e)

Library of Congress Control Number: 2015913276

Print information available on the last page.

WestBow Press rev. date: 9/3/2015

Contents

Foreword

I wish to give special thanks to my wife Frances who have stood with me through many difficult challenges and blessings for over 30 years of marriage. In many ways she has taught me much about what a real leader of influence does.

Special thanks to the congregation that I led as pastor for over 20 years. It was there that I grew as a pastoral leader and allowed me to mature into the leadership style I have today. Special appreciation to the Evangelical Covenant Church denomination in which I served at the national level for 12 years. It was there that I was also challenged to be more of a conceptional and intentional leader. In my over 40 years of serving in para church, local congregations and national level leadership, I have grown to develop a healthy understanding of the kingdom of God and for that I am deeply appreciative.

More about Dr.Donald Davenport

Donald Davenport was born in Chicago Illinois. He sensed a call of God after college to be involved in God's ministry thru various para church Christian organizations. Dr. Davenport previously served as Senior Pastor of the Community Covenant Church in Calumet Park, Illinois for twenty one years. He served on staff in the office of church growth and evangelism in the Evangelical Covenant Church for 12 years.

He is the recipient of several awards. One such example is a Proclamation by the United States Congress for Community Service in 1993 which is filed in the Library of Congress in Washington DC. He was awarded by the Calumet Park Illinois city council, a street sign named in his honor. He recently received the Irving Lambert Award and the Life Time Achievement Award from his denomination, given to those leaders who have made significant contributions in urban ministry in America and the denomination.

Dr Davenport is a member of the American Christian Counseling Association. He has traveled, preached and taught through out the United States and internationally. He attended Southern Illinois University, Garrett Theological Seminary and his PhD in counseling from Bethany Seminary.

Dr Davenport has authored a book "7 Healthy Stages in Male and Female Relationships".It is available online to download as a ebook or purchase in hard copy thru www.amazon.com. He has written booklets on "Transformational Urban Church Planting" and Understanding the Racial Divide in America and the Church"

Dr Davenport has assisted churches across the United States through workshops,seminars and retreats to evolve into a healthy and vibrant church ministries. He continues now in using his gifts in serving as a leadership consultant and counseling for congregations, organizations and marriages in his ministry called Harvest life International.

Dr Davenport is the husband of Frances, a Special Education Consultant. They have been blessed with five children and live in the Chicagoland south suburbs in Illinois.

Introduction

"I will give you shepherds (leadership) after my own heart who will lead you with knowledge and understanding" Jeremiah 3:15 (NIV)

When we say we will act with intention, what actually does that mean? It essentially rises and forms from ones soul. Theologically it is critical to understand that part of the soul of man is the will. The will evolves into a decision and a thirdly it becomes a movement toward an action. Remember, intention is just a mental thought process. A process that determines how and when to get from A to Z. These days when someone is talking about taking positive actions for change they may say they are going do so "with intention" or they are "going to be intentional" about it. Literally, to act with intention means to act with thought only. To act intentionally means to act on purpose. To be intentionally intentional means to act with purpose on your intentions.

This is not just word play or philosophical meanderings. Words do matter. Hopefully this book will assist you to unlock unbounded personal potential opportunities for influence. Someone who is intentionally intentional not only has intentions, they intend to carry them out. The question everyone of us has to ask in leadership is, are the decisions and habits we have today on par with the dreams we have for tomorrow? Listen, here is a secret...it is not going to happen by accident.

Here is how it can be intentionally done:

1.) Set a goal. If you are about to run a race it always helps to know where to find and how to recognize the finish line.
2.) Develop a plan. Without a plan you literally have no idea what you're doing so get that straight.
3.) Start. Good intentions means nothing by itself. Being intentionally intentional means taking action on your intentions.
4.) Build in accountability. Pull people into your plans and have them monitor your progress, or lack of progress. This will keep you motivated and self-assessments will be more honest.
5.) Never quit. Quitting is never an option if you are intentionally intentional. Regrouping, course corrections, redesigns and reboots are not quitting, it always finds a way. No one fails until they quit.

Fully implemented, these steps will ensure that all of your intentions for positive change will begin to take place. That is, if you are intentionally intentional about it. Do you find that some of your good intentions never make it out of the box? Will defining what it means to be intentionally intentional help with your future plans?

One of the valuable truths in life that I have come to learn, if we desire to be successful in leadership, is that we must be live in purpose. When we speak of leadership whether it is in the corporate world, congregational life, community or in the family, it is really about being intentional in our relationships to each other. When a couple decide to get married, it is not enough to go through the marital wedding ceremony and say I do. There has to be a life long commitment to be intentional about how we will strategically decide to love each other.

Listen, being intentional is not just in the macro or big decisions we make but it is also in the micro decisions. If you think about it, we make literally thousands of micro decisions and choices on a daily basis. Just getting out of the bed each day is a decision. We simply decide each day what shoes, pants, dress or even tooth paste we will use. One has to decide to place the keys in the ignition,determine and decide what direction you need to travel. There are literary hundreds of decisions that are made before you finally reach your destination.There are thousands of behaviors on your job, home and relationships that are made on a daily basis. Many of them are conscious and some unconscious decisions and intentions.

The question is are we making the right ones? There has to be a life long commitment to be intentional about how we will strategically decide on how we will live our lives. I have also come to understand that when we decide to live in purpose, it often offends people. It offends because your purpose often conflicts with others often ill conceived assumptions of who you are and how you should lead. Being intentional for the purposes of this book seeks to assist the leader to limit the various distractions and disappointments that often steer the leader to dwell on the dysfunctional margins of leadership.

Leadership is not only about how we get things done. It is not just about getting ideas to completion or accomplishing noble achievements. What gives all of those noble efforts energy and passion is essentially how we relate to each other. The real generic need in all of this is, can I trust you and will I be respected in what I say and contribute. Whether it is in the secular or the religious environment, the culture of an organization, group, home or congregation is critical to the atmosphere of what really motivates us to achieve common goals.

This brief book hopefully will assist you to dig deeper to lead with a intentional heart and lead with understanding to assist in creating a healthy ministry and organizational culture. This book is not to be exhaustive in every aspect in leadership. It hopes to narrow its approach to the character and culture of a group that this leader wish to create and influence. The essential and basic truth is that we all really want to be loved, respected and know that we are valued and that our opinions matter. This process begins with what makes us "tick" and understanding the truth about ourselves as leaders, our style of leadership and what really motivates us.

The scriptures reminds us in Proverbs 20.5 NIV

"The purposes of a mans heart are deep waters, but a man of understanding will draw it out."

The other cogent truth is that we all are leaders in some fashion or other. Dr John Maxwell, the fame leadership guru, tells us that leadership is influence. We all have influence in someone's life or group in some way or another. You may not have been elected or selected officially by any organization but you have some measure of affect and influence on people. It may not necessarily a formal position but it can also be an intentional presence. Here is a humorous example of influence;

Eleven people were hanging on a rope under a helicopter:

10 men and 1 woman. The rope was not strong enough to carry them all so they decided that one had to leave,because otherwise they were all going to fall. They weren't able to choose that one person until the woman gave a very touching speech. She said that she would voluntarily let go of the rope, because, as a woman, she was used to giving up everything for her husband and kids or for men in general, and was used to always making sacrifices with little in return. As soon as she finished her speech, all the men became emotionally overwhelmed and started clapping . . . She was able to influence and achieve her mission. Yes,in many ways influence can be a life or death matter.

The only real question is, what kind of influence are you and are you adding value to the ministry or organization in which you serve. My goal in this book to to assist you to have added leadership value that will assist to create a healthy ministry and group culture. I pray also that in your influence in leadership that God is glorified, because my desire is that you will lead with a heart of God. The Bible tells us of a leader named David who was called a man after God's own heart. He was a young shepherd boy who over time became the king of Israel. He was also a leader with many personal and leadership flaws but in spite of them all he was considered a man after God's own heart. God will use flawed leaders to reach and influence flawed people.

This intentional leader need to know, whether it's fair or unfair, that the atmosphere and culture of the organization essentially begins with them. This person must decide to allow God to craft in their heart God's divine intentions. This person should be one who understands "purpose" and that these purposes and steps should be shaped by God. Proverbs tells us that the steps of a righteous man is ordered by the Lord. The scriptures reminds us in Proverbs 90.12 (NIV) another profound reality about being intentional.

"Teach us to number our days so that we may gain a heart of wisdom"

This reveals that we must also be teachable. In other words there are truths in life that you don't know. It is in these truths as the Gospel of John states, will set you free. In order to know these truths one must be willing to be led by God through other people and circumstances.

This scripture also tells us that leadership understands that the quality of our time on this earth depends upon a heart of wisdom. It understands that everything and every decision should be ordered by God. In many ways this intentional leadership should not only glorify God but also should answer the question what kind of legacy of leadership one wishes to leave behind when their task is complete. When we look at the life of Moses we know that he led a life full of intention but also a life that was directed by the divine intentions of God. In so many ways there are events that visits our lives and they appear to be disappointing and disconnected. But God has a divine way of orchestrating the bends and curves of the roads in our lives for His ultimate purposes.

Such was the case with Moses. God intentionally took Moses out of where he was to where his destiny as a leader would be. For example, in Exodus Chapter 1 Pharaoh made a declaration that all Hebrew new born babies would be killed. Moses mother sought to hide him along the reeds on the bank of the Nile River in order to save his life. Pharaoh's daughter saw the child while bathing one day and gave this child favor and raised him as her own in the same house of the one who tried to kill him. We see in this same story how Moses mother, in God's providential intentions, was used to nurse this baby and received payment for nursing him! Yes, there is often a paradox and irony in God's intentional will for our lives.

You need to know that often God's providence will place you in unusual places of privilege to position you intentionally for the next level of blessing and purpose in your life. God's intentional design is further seen when Moses, as he got older, was providentially drawn out of the palace to flee for his life because he killed an Egyptian when he was trying to defend one of his fellow Hebrew brothers. Moses fled to Midian to escape because the Egyptian police was seeking to capture him. Over time and through many circumstances God continued to intentionally lead Moses to His purposes to eventually give leadership to lead his people out of the oppression of Egypt. The purpose of God eventually and intentionally led Moses out of Egypt and an enslaved nation eventually found its way to the land of promise. This was a fulfillment of a promise He gave to Abraham centuries earlier.

Moses name essentially mean to be drawn out. Sometimes your birth and purposes are not just where you were but rather where you will be. It's not always who you are now but who you shall be and like Moses,drawn out to become later. Your question today is, are the habits you have today on par with the dreams you have for tomorrow? Let's look at the intentional sequence of Moses again,

Moses was...
Drawn out of his mother womb...
Drawn out of the river
Drawn out of the palace
Drawn to a burning bush so that God can give him the call to leadership
Drawn out of slavery thru another set of waters...red sea
Drawn out to receive directions in the form of the 10 Commandments to provide order

When we live an intentional life, God takes what was hidden in you and exposes your gifts in public so that those we serve in leadership can be informed and transformed. God gave Moses the 10 commandments not the 10 suggestions as an intentional guideline for the people to live out the proper behaviors in order to co exist and receive successfully all of the blessings and opportunities of what was ahead of them in the land of promise. Moses left a leadership legacy that when he died God said in Deuteronomy 34.10-12 (NIV)

"Since then no prophet has risen in Israel like Moses, whom the Lord knew face to face, who did all those miraculous signs and wonders The Lord sent him to do in Egypt...to Pharaoh and to all his officials and to his whole land. For no one has ever shown the mighty power or performed the awesome deeds that Moses did in the sight of all Israel."

When I read these verses, I found myself amazed and deeply awed of what God is able to do through us if we simply surrender behaviors and attitudes that are not healthy in leading his people. Yes, His people and not your people. Sometimes this may mean God allowing us to travel through places and discussions of discomfort in order to stretch and mold us. God comforts the afflicted but He also afflicts the comfortable. It is God's desire that we lead his people and not drive his people. We are to be shepherd leaders leading sheep ......not cattle herders with a proverbial whip driving bulls and cows.

Through this simple book we will seek what it means to be an intentional leader through 7 intentions below

1. Intentionally Capacious - Expanding and growing beyond my level of comfort
2. Intentionally Collaborative - Knowing that one of us is never greater than all of us
3. Intentionally Challenging - Standing tall in the midst of conflict
4. Intentionally Compassionate - Connecting and empathetic to the people you serve
5. Intentionally Communicative - Clarifying the vision, values and the expectations of the mission
6. Intentionally Conscious - Being aware of the environment around me and my limitations.
7. Intentionally Called - Sensing that this is more than what I do but more of my purpose

CHAPTER 1

The Intentional Capacious Leader

Expanding and growing beyond our level of comfort

The word "capacious" is word that essentially and simply means one who is in a continual state of growing,expanding and learning. The intentional leader in order to be effective has to develop a clear understanding of the value of being capacious. In many ways this begins when one appreciates and has a true sense of "veritas". This word is from the Latin language, simply meaning truth. In Roman mythology this was the goddess of truth. She was the daughter of Saturn and the mother of Virtue. We see this word veritas as a motto inscribed inside of a shield in many of our academic institutions such as colleges and universities. You may wonder why is this so important in the life of a leader? The truth about who we really are essentially reveals and unleashes the condition of our hearts. The bible tells us that "from the heart flows the issues of life". Our purpose in this book is to look not only at the strategic value of a leader but also more of the veritas or truths of a leader's intrinsic interior life.

When I think upon my years leadership, the unspoken question I believe people were asking within themselves on choosing to follow me was "Do I like him", "Is he likable", or "Is he someone

I can trust with my life and family". Maybe they are also asking "Can he lead with integrity?" The bible gives us cogent insight into this.

"David shepherded (led) them with integrity of heart and with skilled hands he led them" (Psalm 78:72 NIV)

The New Living Bible translate this verse this way.
"He cared for them with a true heart and led them with skillful hands"

This Capacious leader has to focus on 10 intentional skillful hands abilities that are critical green flags in order to give effective and efficient leadership;

- The ability to maintain personal, professional and spiritual balance in their life.
- The ability to motivate and develop leaders concerning their purpose.
- The ability to motivate by communicating a clear clear vision.
- The ability to integrity their present reality and lead change.
- The ability to promote and lead leadership formation in your ministry or group.
- The ability to provide and initiate a high relevant worship experience (if you are a pastor)
- The ability to identify, develop and support leaders around you.
- The ability to build, inspire and lead a team of both staff and volunteers.
- The ability to manage conflict

- The ability to navigate successfully in the ever expanding world of technology.

When a leader is in a constant and continual state of growing into the truth about themselves they create a culture in their environment of transparency and community. The question is how do a leader begin to create the necessary skills to make this happen? Let's look at 4 capacious growth values that becomes the seeds planted in a leaders spirit to make this happen.

- One who has integrity
- One who is adaptive
- One who is clear in their identity
- One who has the right passion

INTEGRITY

The fame author and thought leader Dr Deepak Chopra has a interesting comment about today's leaders who are specifically leaders of countries. He says that these leaders are essentially persons who are held in captivity by self interest groups. In other words the people who got them in office and financed their campaigns will influence their decisions toward these same people's self interest. This is a challenge for those who wish to lead with integrity at the macro level. Let's look at another person who struggled with integrity at the micro areas of life. A 42-year-old Cicero Illinois man stole credit cards and unopened presents during two recent burglaries in a town in Riverside Illinois, then re-wrapped the gifts and put them under his own Christmas tree for friends and family, police report said. He was willing to take something that didn't belong to him to receive approval. He did a good thing in giving gifts but how he did it lacked integrity. Integrity asks "can God trust you when no one is watching?"

This example essentially believes that the end justifies the end. If a leader leads a ministry with this type of logic without any conscience or principles, this could prove problematic in leadership. This could essentially could affect a very precious gift of trust that a group would have in a leader. If trust is gone it affects the culture of the home, group, church and organization. The bible in the books of Acts tells of a married couple named Ananias and Sapphiras. This is a story of trust and their personal possessions. They made a promise to sell their land and give the profits to the disciples for the work of the ministry. In reality what they did was sell the land but kept part of the profits but didn't live in integrity because they didn't tell the leadership all that they did. They were soon exposed and disciplined. They never recovered from their decision, because their choice ended in their death.

Perhaps the most common integrity issue is to lie and tell ourselves I can do things in less time than I actually can. But lying to ourselves in this way sets us up to lie to others. How many times have you told your love one that you would arrive at a certain time and place when in your heart you wasn't genuinely committed to following through on your word? You told them that you would be there, but you wasn't. They soon learn not to trust you, because your actions don't always line up with your words. To justify ourselves we view our tardiness as a minor character flaw. In other words, we like to be untruthful about the selfishness that characterizes our way of managing time. This could prove problematic in leading a organization or group.

One who desires to be capacious and grow understands that their words has to line up with their actions. We saw in the previous illustration that this wasn't the case. A leader's word is their bond and often establishes the type of a culture that this group will become. This leader has to grow to be transparent and not hesitant to admit their weakness and flaws before those they serve. This is not to say that this is natural for us to do. The benefit of this behavior is that those who observe this behavior will soon realize that they too can live in transparency and admit their flaws.

The bible tells of another person in Genesis 39 named Joseph.

As you read his story you will see that in all of his challenges and disappointments he maintained his integrity. In other words living in obedience to his sense of what is right and what he could personally live with. It was through his skillful and steadfast behavior that created the pathway for Joseph to become a influential leader. The scriptures tells us that through all of the set backs and obstacles Joseph went through, he knew God was with him. When a leader fully understands their purpose and the God who is leading them,nothing gets in the way of their faith and the purposes God has for them. They may get redirected but never lost.

There are moments in leadership where what is before us becomes blurred and if one is not careful they will find themselves and their ministry drifting and being negatively affected from their diminishing sense of integrity.

Here are possible 4 signs of drifting in this area

- When a leader is faced with continual chronic conflicts within him or herself and within the group. This may be because of their limited ministry skill set to bring resolution and peace.
- When sin and inappropriate behaviors are tolerated by the leader which creates unintended consequences of factions,divisions and discontent.
- When the leader is struggling with personal temptations or family issues and it is affecting their ability to lead their ministry effectively
- When people begin to say to the leader"things have been tense around here for a while"

One of our greatest Presidents Abraham Lincoln wrote about integrity in leadership when we find ourselves with no answers.

"I have been driven many times upon my knees by the overwhelming conviction that I had no where else to go. My own wisdom and that all about me, insufficient for the day"

ADAPTIVE

The next area for this capacious leader is their ability to be adaptive. This simply means the wisdom of a leader to discern when to adjust to the new realities around them in healthy ways.

The scriptures reminds us in Romans 12:1-2 that this adaptive behavior begins with a mind that is renewed.

Therefore, I urge you, brothers and sisters, in view of God's mercy, to offer your bodies as a living sacrifice, holy and pleasing to God—this is your true and proper worship. Do not conform to the pattern of this world, but be transformed by the renewing of your mind. Then you will be able to test and approve what God's will is—his good, pleasing and perfect will. (Romans 12:1-2 NIV)

A renewed mind is always in a constant state of being adaptive and discerning God's will for a situation. It adapts because situations and events in the life of a organization often changes. However what changes are not the values and principles that are embedded in our faith but rather how they are packaged and presented. It is how we appropriate the strategy and process so that God is ultimately honored.

I do know that the sin of stubbornness and pride often gets in the way of being adaptive. Abraham received a mission from God in Genesis 12 to leave where he was in a land called Ur of Chaldea. God wanted him to move out of his comfort zone and journey to another place that He designed in order to give leadership to a new people and a new promise. This would be for a promise that Abraham will never experience himself. His call was to be one of obedience even though the promise was to be experienced by others generations later. It is often difficult for some people to live in obedience when the fruits and benefits of your labor will be experienced by others in the future.

It is not always easy dealing with being adaptive. Sometimes the struggle in adaptability is confronting what Abraham must have struggled with. For him it was the idea of moving from what was familiar to what was unfamiliar. From comfort to discomfort. It was the idea of not fully knowing. If one has a personality that is controlling and doesn't like surprises, this would be a difficult journey to take. God sometimes will take us from our level of comfort to a place of discomfort in order to eventually at the right time provide comfort and provision for others.

Consider a pastoral leader who was struggling with a change in their personal life.

"We are considering a move. Sensing that God may be leading us to sell our home and see what is next. I know that the most practical people in my life would worry about such a decision. But it is what we sense. Last year God began to encourage us to learn the difference between trust and clarity. I am notoriously one who prefers clarity. I am willing to do whatever God makes clear, but that does not seem to be God's goal for us these days. Instead he is taking us deeper into trust. I realize that many people don't quite understand this. I was recently with a church group and asked for prayer - not for clarity but for trust. Immediately the group switched and insisted that clarity was what I needed. Good intentioned as that was, I am learning the gentle pressure of the Spirit to simply walk where the path seems to go and to trust that the path maker will shape its director. This is hard and the process sometime gets harder"

I wonder if Abraham must have felt like this when he received his unusual call from God to leave Ur. Being adaptable is not easy. Adjusting to what God is saying and how he is moving us means a constant state of saying God this is new to me but I am trusting you because you see the promise more than I can see the present.

In a ministry group the mindset that is in renewal, capacious and adaptable senses when the ministry is drifting and struggling when:

- When the leader is unable to adapt the ministry to the changing realities in the church and community they serve.
- When the leader is expressing needs of the ministry that are either being ignored or there is an inability to meet the the evolving needs before them.
- When the leader's teaching and instructions are not meeting the felt needs of the group.
- When the people begin to chatter, "when will things begin to change or when will the leadership do something"

PASSION

The third area of a capacious leader is one that has passion. This is more in line with the idea of desire. This is a internal drive that thirst and hunger to do the will of God. They sense a call that is greater than themselves. Some may say that this person has a heart for the things that God has passion about. The bible tells us that David, who rose from a shepherd boy to a King, was Man after God's own heart. We read in Psalm 63.1(NIV)

"You God are my God, earnestly I seek you; I thirst for you, my whole being longs for you, in a dry and parched land where there is no water"

When a leader has a heart for God they will in turn have a heart for God's people. People that you serve know the difference between whether you care for them or what they can do for you. The Bible tells of a man named Nehemiah who had a comfortable position in the palace as a cup bearer for the King. When he heard about the horrible conditions of his country concerning the wall of Jerusalem broken down and the gates burned with fire he had to look deep within himself. He began to recognize that his position in the palace was not as important as his passion for God and His people. We read in Nehemiah Chapter 1 that when he heard these things he sat down and wept. In fact for many days mourned prayed and fasted. He then gave a long passionate prayer to God, calling upon Him to remember his covenant and to bring back restoration to his people. A capacious person with passion always drives him to a mission to restore and expand the work of God. When people see this in a leader they will be infected and affected by his fire and passionately follow as the Israelites followed Nehemiah.

One can determine if they have a intentionally passionate spirit by checking out the signs below;

- I find myself waking up in the morning clearly knowing God's call on my life.
- I have a true sense of God's plan for my life
- I sense that others are drawn to me because of my sense of purpose.
- I am constantly thinking of ways to get others to join me in what I am doing.
- I find myself dreaming regularly about the mission God has for me.
- I get excited when I hear others talk about the things that God is doing.
- I find myself reading books etc about the work that I am presently in.

- God has given me a clear vision for what I am doing for Him,
- I am always thinking about ways to improve and expand the work.
- People tell me that my teaching and speaking is inspiring.

What are some of the signs of gradual, decline and drifting? How do we begin to know when the leadership and group is in a period of stagnation?

- When the leader discerns that there is a feeling of lethargy in his heart and a loss of momentum in the culture of the congregation and leadership.
- When the leader begins to see what they do more of a job and there is slow diminishing joy in what they are doing.
- When a leader over time has been losing their desire to serve in the present ministry and has constant thoughts of another occupation or serving in another ministry. There is a sense that the "air is coming out of their balloon".
- When the leader begin to say and ask "what happened to the fire and joy in this ministry that I serve?

IDENTITY

The last area of a growing capacious leader is their sense of identity. This is critical in the life of a leader who desires to be intentional about their leadership. Knowing who you are and your style of leadership is very important in the life and culture of a organization or ministry.The scriptures tells us of a man name Gideon in Judges 6 and 7. He was not seeking leadership until God confronted him while he was hiding and gave him an new identity. The people of Israel were oppressed by the Midianites. In fact the scriptures tells us that they so impoverished the Israelites that they cried out to The Lord for help. The story goes on to tell us that Gideon was so scared that he hid and threshed wheat in a wine press to keep it from the Midianites. In other words Gideon was so frightened that he was using something out of its normal purpose. He was hiding in a wine press to keep the wheat he needed to make bread in fear of it being from taken from him. There are too many potential leaders hiding in the wine press of churches and organizations who are out of position to be used of God. They are often living in fear that their time, life and resources, like the wheat, will being taken from them. In Gideon's case God divinely intervened and speaks to him about who he really is and the mission that is before him. In other words God sees in each of us much more than we see in ourselves. We see fear but God sees your future. We see failure but God sees the victory ahead.

Judges 6:11-12 (NIV)
"The angel of The Lord came and sat down under the oak in Ophrah that belong to Joash the Abiezrite, where his Son Gideon was threshing wheat in a wine press to keep it from the Midianites. When the angel of The Lord appeared to Gideon, he said, "The Lord is with you, Mighty Warrior"

What is so amazing is that next we see a angel appearing to Gideon. The angel tells him, The Lord is with you, *mighty warrior.* At this point he is anything but a warrior. He is in hiding and in fear for his sustenance and life. We see again that even in our short sighted fears God's grace sees in us what we are unable to see in ourselves. God saw the identity of a warrior, a fighter and one who has skill set and ability to give intentional leadership.

When Gideon believed this about himself only then was he able to lead his people from a moment to a movement to a significant victory over the Midianites. When he understood his identity and what God said about him, this gave him renewed confidence and made him intentional about how he needed to lead. When we understand our identity, what God says about us and who we are in Christ we will receive renewed insight into the journey of grace that is waiting for us.

How do we know when we are clear about our identity?. Let's look at some intentional indicators to assist us;

- I find myself waking up in the morning clearly knowing God's will for my life.
- I sense that others are drawn to me because of my sense do purpose.
- I don't find myself distracted by what the successes or failures of other people.
- I Sometimes feel so comfortable about what I am doing that I never really feel I am working
- I am clear about what God has called me to do
- I find myself assisting others to understand their calling
- I find myself going to working excited about what God will do today.
- I have a clear understanding in my life and walk with God.

One of the things that I believe we need to do, as leaders, is have a continual assessment about who we are. In many ways we can find ourselves drifting from our identity as a organization and ministry over time. Below are four areas that can assist in this process;

- When the leader is not clear on their role and purpose
- When the leader has not developed clear demarcations between their personal life and public ministry.
- When the leader and church ministry vision and values are not impacting the lives of the people they wish to serve.
- When the leader reflects and begins to say "what have I become? How did I wind up here? Nothing is being accomplished.

The Capacious leader seeks to be intentional in the growing edges areas of being a person of integrity, identity, passion and becoming adaptive.

CHAPTER 2

The Intentional Leader is Collaborative

Knowing that one of us is never greater than all of us

There is an African proverb that states "if you wish to go fast go alone but if you wish to go far go together". A person who desires to be an intentional leader who desires to go far together with their group need to understand and seek the necessity of agreement. These leaders know that collaboration seeks the foundation of agreement because of their common faith as believers. They fully understand what Jesus says about when two or three are gathered in his name that he will be in their midst. They also understand their own personal leadership strengths and weaknesses. They seek to move in partnership recognizing the gifts in others in order to get things done for the kingdom. Self centered leaders are a threat to collaboration and often find themselves in an unending vortex of conflict. Wise and other centered collaborators truly understand that team work makes a dream work.

In the sport of football, the quarterback is the leader of the team but he knows he is only as effective as the team of players of around him. The quarterback knows the value of pulling the offensive team together to collaborate after each play. He calls the play and every one knows their assignment based upon their position. If the quarterback doesn't work with his team, he will find that there is no one to hand the ball off to, no linemen to block for him and no receivers to throw the ball to. Just like in the sports world, a leader knows that some times it is not always the team that has the best players that win. It is the team who plays the best and is intentionally collaborative that is often successful. The team is intentionally collaborative because they have studied the playbook and they have had collaborative times to coordinate and go over the plays together thru practice.

The scriptures tells us a interesting reality in Matthew 18:20

"For where two or three are gathered together in my name, there I am with them"

There are three key distinctive realities from this verse that initiates intentional collaboration

- When there is more than one of us
- When we come together for the purposes of Him
- When these are present Christ is embedded with them

When a person who seeks to be collaborative understands this they create the initial environment for success and a healthy organizational culture. They know the danger of going forth alone and the danger of exposing themselves to the realities of ministry isolation. The collaborative person knows that they serve as a servant to the group and that the people they serve in turn feels truly invested and provides the leader with wise counsel and cooperation.

Proverbs 11:14 (NIV)
For lack of guidance a nation falls but many advisors makes a victory sure

There is an African word "Ubuntu" it means I am because you are. There is a sense that we are deeply rooted and connected together. This principle of caring for each other's well being is promoted and celebrated in the culture of the organization. Each individual's humanity is ideally expressed through his or her relationship with others.

A person with a Ubuntu mindset is a leader who is welcoming, hospitable, warm and generous. These leaders are open and available to others and do not feel threaten that others maybe more skilled and competent. In fact they welcome those who are more skilled and competent to serve around them. They have a self assurance that comes from knowing that they belong and interconnected to a greater good. They know that they are diminished when others are humiliated and diminished when others are treated as if they have little value to the group. Ubuntu creates a healthy culture within the group and organization to move toward the power of agreement.

The Collaboration of Sequoia trees

One occasion in California I notice these tall trees in Yosemite National Park called Sequoias. They are the world's largest single tree and grow to an average height of 164-274 ft tall and 20-26 ft in diameter. I further noticed that their roots were barely above the surface of the ground. I asked the person I was with how can you have tall trees still standing and the roots are barely above surface! A strong wind can come and blow these trees over. He indicated that these trees grow only in groves and their roots intertwine under the surface of the earth. So when the strong winds come, they will hold each other up. The lesson for me in this was that in the same way family, friends, church body and other groups should be intertwine like groves so that when strong winds of life and inter group conflicts blow, these people like the roots of the Sequoia trees can serve as reinforcement and hold each other up. Real collaboration in ministry can provide the same benefit and value.

Collaboration acknowledges both the rights and the res-ponsibilities of every person in the group or ministry. It seeks this through knowing that every individual has an equal say in any discussion and on ultimately reaching an agreement that is acceptable to all. The intentional leader who is in collaboration, skillfully leads without dominating or being perceived as controlling. To be clear this isn't a waving of the white flag surrendering ones leadership. My proposition here is that the contrary is taking place. Strong leadership begins through carefully, firmly guiding and releasing others to build healthy effective group dynamics.

Collaborating to Change Group Momentum

When we look in the bible we notice again Nehemiah. He needed to restore not just a city but a people in shambles. He understood he had to get the people to move together in a common cause. There are 10 reasons why ministries and organizations fail.

- Not collaborating first with God in prayer. One subtle mistake leaders unlike Nehemiah, often makes is not going and laboring before God in fasting and prayer. He sought God before he sought and went before the people.

- Allowing too much complacency. The biggest mistake when trying to change is to plunge in without establishing a high sense of urgency in the people they serve.
- Failing to collaborate in building coalition for movement. Major change is impossible unless the leaders are supporting the new direction.
- Failure to communicate and collaborate the power of vision. Vision plays a key role in producing useful change by helping to direct align and inspire action on the part of people.
- Under communicating the vision together. People will not make sacrifices, even if they are unhappy with the status quote, unless they believe the potential benefits of change are attractive and if they believe that this is even achievable. Unless the leader is collaborating through communication, people's hearts and minds are never captured.
- Lack of collaboration permits obstacles to block the vision. If they feel disempowered, this will create unintended stumbling blocks to move forward.
- Collaboration allows the group to move forward and be realistic to create short term wins. This will maintain momentum for the long term goals.
- Collaboration with everyone involve provides the right culture and environment
- Collaboration creates the connectional glue that allows the group to see and understand the power of evil. There are forces of darkness that wish to disrupt the mission.

- Collaboration reminds the leader that this work is much bigger than themselves. There should be a continual seeking of peer input and mentoring.

Are you a Collaborative Leader?

Essentially, one will recognize this by leading by example, embracing vulnerability, and having a strong belief in sharing.

Leading by Example

In the Old Testament we read much about shepherds. When we carefully observe this we understand that they usually led from the rear of a flock of sheep. We can translate this to mean for our times and purposes, leaders also can carefully lead their organizations or groups from behind. This sounds very counter intuitive doesn't it? You would think one would lead from the front. A shepherd strategically led in two ways. He led positionally and provisionally. It was just as important for the shepherd positionally see the state and challenges of what the sheep faced as they went forward. It was also important for the shepherd to provisionally lead. He had to skillfully used his rod to motivate sheep to move forward but also the staff for protection to pull back a sheep who may be wandering. The leader know that they are not managers who come in after a plan or process is completed and merely approve and support the budget. Shepherd leaders know that collaboration is skillfully woven in being an example through rolling up their sleeves and involving themselves in the process of group ownership. Remember, the closeness of his leadership with the sheep was such that often the shepherd smelled like the sheep they led at the end of their day.

Embracing Vulnerability

This goes hand and hand with being transparent. Too many of our organizations were modeled after the military and if there is one thing a commander wasn't, and that was being vulnerable. However times have changed and we aren't running our organizations like the military anymore. We go through our whole lives learning how to be the opposite of vulnerable and we tend to have a shield up to keep people from seeing us when we are vulnerable. There are times when we are afraid and don't know what to do next. Your group may need to hear this from you. Vulnerability is about having the courage to show up and remove facades that hides our frailties.

Belief in Sharing

Traditional leaders would sit at the top of the organization or ministry and had access to all of the information required to make decisions. This leader would act as a top down manager who would dole out the orders and the team would execute the orders without asking any questions. The collaborative leader doesn't believe in hoarding information. They share information and collective intelligence. They believe the whole is greater than its parts. A leader would be surprise if they only release. They would see how the affirmation of their authority will come back to them.

These leaders also makes sure that others connect with each other and the information they need to get the job done, anytime,anywhere and on any device. In the old world of silos and solo players, leaders had access to everything they needed under one roof and a command style served them well. But things have changed. The world has become much more interconnected, and if leaders don't know how to tap into the power of those connections, they will live in disappointment. The Holy Spirit in collaboration through the scriptures tells us that we are to equip the saints for the work of the ministry. In other words provide them with the necessary tools and information so that effective and efficient work can be jointly achieved.

It is also important that this collaborative person lead with a strong hand. They know that working smarter is often better than working harder. The other reality is that once we begin to collaborate they potentially can face a different challenge. They can overdo it. Too often people will try to collaborate on everything and wind up in endless meetings, debating ideas and struggling to find consensus. They can't reach decisions and execute quickly. Collaboration at this point becomes not the oil greasing the wheel but the sand grinding it to a halt.

Becoming a Link

In his best selling book "The Tipping Point" Malcolm Gladwell used the term connector to describe individuals who have many ties to different social worlds. It's not the number of people they know that makes the connectors significant, however, it's their ability to link people, ideas and resources that wouldn't normally bump into one another. In churches, businesses etc, connectors are critical facilitators of collaboration.

There is a president of a well known technology company. He knows the value of being a connector because of the value it brings. He spends much of his time traveling around the world to meet people, partners, customers. He knows that in collaboration he needs to spend time with media owners to hear what they think about digital platforms, Facebook and pricing models. He needs to get their views on new technologies. He says these conversations lead to new strategic insights and relationships to assist his company to expand. Collaboration of this kind raises the value and brand of their organization.

In the same way Christian leaders would be wise to know that their mission and work expands when they are connecting and collaborating with others who may have insights and cutting edge views that will assist the group and organization to be more successful.

Collaborative Style is Pragmatic Leadership

The most efficient way to lead, if you want to be completely pragmatic about it, is via dictatorship. A system in which one person makes all the autonomous decisions is, at least for a while, the most efficient, the least messy. But power corrupts, and ultimately, while decisions get made and orders are carried out, those decisions are often bad ones. Great execution of a bad decision is still, well, a mess. Dictatorship, even benevolent dictatorship, is neither healthy nor biblical.

The difference between "do it this way!" and "What if we did it this way?" is subtle but important. One of our greatest ways to influence the church is by modeling collaborative leadership, which is what all believers—men and women—are called to in the New Testament. Listen, leadership that builds consensus and collaboration does not necessarily come naturally to anyone, male or female. We are all human beings and therefore, at least a little selfish. We all need to improve our skills in collaborative leadership.

There is a New Testament word that point clearly toward collaboration and cooperation. This style of leadership does not compromise authority, but reflects the beautiful mutual submission that the Bible calls us to live in.mJesus told his disciples:

"So now I am giving you a new commandment: Love each other. Just as I have loved you, you should love each other" (John 13:34 NIV).

The word translated "each other" in this pivotal verse is "allelon". Also translated "one another," this Greek word appears 100 times in the New Testament. We find it scattered in the epistles, coupled with exhortations regarding what we should do: pray for, love, serve, comfort, encourage…each other.

For example: "Love each other with genuine affection, and take delight in honoring each other" (Romans 12:10 NIV). It's also in these verses that remind us what we should not do: judge, speak unkindly, lie. For example: "So let's stop condemning each other. Decide instead to live in such a way that you will not cause another believer to stumble and fall" (Romans 14:13 NIV).The word "allelon" in the Greek language expresses the mutuality and community that is an inextricable part of our faith. Christianity is a one-another faith, and as leaders, we are to model that orientation of collaboration toward others.

CHAPTER 3

The Intentional Leader is Prepared for Challenge

Standing tall in the midst of conflict

The challenge of Intentional leadership is what often comes once the honeymoon in leadership period ends. Notice I said challenge and not problem of leadership. It is a problem when we don't trust God for the outcome and we try to figure it out on our own limited vision. It is a challenge when we know that God is leading, guiding and teaching in the midst of the journey. The challenge for the Intentional leader is not what she or he is confronted with, it is their response to the challenge that determine how the culture of that group thrives long afterwards. This leader understands that opposition and obstruction has a way of finding its way in their journey in giving leadership. They are not surprised and they choose to see these two challenges of opposition and obstruction as normal and natural.

Let's look at 1 Peter 4:12 (NIV)

Dear friends (leaders) do not be surprised at the fiery ordeals that come on to you to test you as though something is strange were happening to you.

I believe a wise leader prepares and gets ahead of the challenges that faces every leader. They prepare through studying and looking at the scriptures of those who found themselves in the middle of opposition. Look at Nehemiah as one of the sources for preparation.

Nehemiah Chapters 4:1-6

But it so happened, when Sanballat heard that we were rebuilding the wall, that he was furious and very indignant, and mocked the Jews. And he spoke before his brethren and the army of Samaria, and said, "What are these feeble Jews doing? Will they fortify themselves? Will they offer sacrifices? Will they complete it in a day? Will they revive the stones from the heaps of rubbish— stones that are burned?" Now Tobiah the Ammonite was beside him, and he said, "Whatever they build, if even a fox goes up on it, he will break down their stone wall." Hear, O our God, for we are despised; turn their reproach on their own heads, and give them as plunder to a land of captivity! Do not cover their iniquity, and do not let their sin be blotted out from before You; for they have provoked You to anger before the builders. So we built the wall, and the entire wall was joined together up to half its height, for the people had a mind to work. (Nehemiah 4:1-6 NKJV)

This statement below is heard in many churches

"This is the most abominable church I have ever seen. It breaks my heart that you lead so many children away from God. You should all be ashamed of yourselves. You call yourselves Christians but I doubt you even know who Christ is. I will never come to this Satan's den again!"

Those not so encouraging comments were written on the back of a roll call card by a visitor to a church years ago. Since she left only her first name and no address or phone number there was no opportunity to discuss her concerns. She just vented her caustic criticism at a time when dozens were coming to Christ every week and the Spirit of God was really at work in this particular church.

Coping with criticism has always been a big challenge for leaders. When Nehemiah began to rebuild the wall around Jerusalem he was the target of a series of vicious attacks from two self-appointed critics: Sanballat and Tobiah. These local dissidents ridiculed the quality of his work, "Even if a fox climbed up on it, he would break down their wall of stones!" Nehemiah didn't respond to them. He just prayed, "O God, turn their insults back on their own heads." And the people continued to work with all their heart.

The critics then asked Nehemiah to stop building temporarily and attend a meeting to discuss the wisdom of the project. Nehemiah declined saying, "I am carrying on a great project and cannot go down." The disturbed adversaries then circulated false rumors that Nehemiah was planning an armed revolt and was motivated by a lust for power. They accused him of plotting to be king. Nehemiah replied, "Nothing like what you are saying is happening; you are just making it up out of your head."

Sanballat and Tobiah even hired a hit man to kill him but Nehemiah refused to be intimidated and he just kept on building. He prayed fervently that God would protect him and deal with his detractors.

Nehemiah's experience teaches several intentional lessons to all leaders in challenge:

Be realistic

Criticism is inevitable no matter how noble your deed or significant your achievement. Nehemiah should have been above criticism. His project was needed, his motives were pure, his leadership was superb, and he was receiving no personal remuneration or special recognition. Yet he was the victim of ruthless attacks.

Be discerning

Seek to understand the motives behind the criticism. Some scrutiny is valid and healthy. Solomon wrote, "He who listens to a life-giving rebuke will be at home among the wise" (Proverbs 15:31 NIV). But the criticism leveled at Nehemiah wasn't honest or constructive. His detractors wanted the project to fail.

Be cautious

Not all criticism should be answered. The initial reaction is to answer every stupid accusation. But Nehemiah ignored some of the objections and answered others. To determine our reaction it helps to ask a series of questions. Is the criticism sincere or is the critic just venting anger? Will answering the criticism help the project or do more damage by keeping the issue alive? Is this the first reply or are we rehashing old arguments? Is the criticism reasonable or are we giving credibility to a perverse attack by answering it? Does answering help others or am I just defending myself?

Be prayerful

Talk to God before talking to the critic. Nehemiah asked for God's intervention and wisdom. When we ask for God's help we're more likely to be objective and less likely to respond in anger.

Be focused

Don't allow criticism to cloud the big picture. Nehemiah stayed on task and when he did respond his answers were brief and to the point. He refused to be detracted from his lofty mission. The result? "So the wall was completed...in fifty two days. When all our enemies heard about his, all the surrounding nations were afraid and lost their self-confidence, because they realized that his work had been done with the help of our God" (Nehemiah 6:15-16).

The Intentional Challenges a Leader Faces as they Lead

The Intentional Leader knows and understand the nature and tentacles of challenge. Rev Pete Scazzero in his book the "Emotionally Healthy Church" states 8 challenges of a leader.

1. Dual Relationships- Supervision and Being Friends

We are a church family and we often hire our friends who then become our employees. The result is I become both your pastor/spiritual leader/supervisor and friend. Which is it? We hire people we mentor and then they become our employees with a contractual agreement and money is exchanged. We are naïve to admit that all things are equal. They are not when we have the power to fire or increase/decrease someone's pay. The people we lead do not have the same power over us. Friends enjoy an equal power relationship. Dual relationships create countless opportunities for misunderstandings. Am I saying, "Don't ever do it?" No, just do it with your eyes open. The risk is enormous. Failures and broken friendships abound in church leaderships around the world.

2. Hiring/Firing and Being a Church Family

This is perhaps our most difficult challenge as church leaders. To terminate a person in the corporate world is painful. In a church setting, it is excruciating. We became pastors and leaders to serve and help people, not hurt them. Yet if we don't steward God's resources well by hiring and firing well, we betray our people who trust we are leading well and doing the right thing.

3. Strategic Planning and Waiting on God

Balancing the process of goal setting and the strategic planning process with prayerful discernment is no small task. What is God saying? What season are we in as a church/organization? What is God's will for us? The fact that a door is open and we can do something does not mean it is His will for us now. Jesus struggled with the will of the Father in the Garden of Gethsemane. He had to submit his will to the Father. How much more do we?

4. Preaching/Teaching and Our Integrity

It is easy to preach and teach what we are not living. People trust that we have spent time with God in prayer and stillness to speak for Him publicly. People trust we are living what we are preaching and teaching. If we can't say "Imitate me as I imitate Christ," then we need to press the pause button. Investing time in our development and growth is perhaps the greatest contribution we make to our teaching and to our people.

5. Leading the Church and the Marriage Vow

Ephesians 5:32 argues that our earthly marriage is a pointer of something beyond itself – of the profound mystery of Christ's marriage to His bride, the church. Our marriage, if we are married, is our most powerful message to our churches. It is a sacrament, imaging something invisible. The marriage vow is both a limit and a gift. Like a monastic vow it informs all we do and every decision we make every day. To expand our churches as a leader as if we were single is a violation of Scripture and our vows.

6. Social Media/Technology and the Ancient Church

God has called us, like the apostle Paul, to contextualize the gospel and bring Christ to our culture. That culture today is Twitter, blogging, Facebook and the worldwide web. At the same time we learn from the great cloud of witnesses who have preceded us. We learn from church history and the early church fathers (e.g. Ignatius of Antioch, Athanasius, Cyril of Alexandria, Basil, Gregory the Great, Augustine) who were leaders of local churches, theologians, and monks who prayed their theology. We are called to be an "Ancient/Future Church."

7. The Gift of Limits and Casting Vision

The issue of limits touches the core of our tendency to do our will not God's, to rebel rather than submit, to grasp rather than surrender. Adam and Eve violated God's limits. Jesus submitted to the Father's in the wilderness. We are called to lead our people into the God's future. We carry the tension however, that we easily can take over Gods' work for Him, violate His protective gifts of limits, and unleash chaos into our churches. Remember the bible teaches that without a vision, the people will perish.

8. Listening to God in Our Losses and Leading by Faith

In every church, relationships end, ministries die, dreams dissipate and leaders move on. Jeremiah, Jesus, Job, and David had a full-orbed theology for the disorientation that comes with loss and grieving. Integrating this into our Western church culture of leadership that is always growing and expanding to take the next hill is problematic. We are called to lead our people forward. The discernment question is whether that means leading them to listen to God internally first before moving into the next new initiative.

The challenge of leaders within the walls of a church

The challenges of every Leader are often challenges within the church or a specific organization within it. Some even call these churches "mean" and this perception is seen as a negative witness to the community it seeks to serve. Their growth is stagnated and are usually the last ones to come to the reality of their poor witness.

1. Too many decisions are made in the cloak of darkness. Only a select few members really know what's going on. The attitude of those elitists is that the typical member doesn't really need to know.

2. The pastor and/or staff are treated poorly. Decisions are made about them without a fair process. Complaints are often numerous and veiled. Many of these churches are known for firing pastors and/or staff with little apparent cause.

3. Power groups tenaciously hold on to their power. The power group may be a formal group such as a committee, elders, or deacons. But the group can also be informal—no official role but great informal authority. Power groups avoid and detest accountability, which leads to the next point.

4. There is lack of clear accountability for major decisions and/or expenditures. The church has no clear system in place to make certain that a few outlier members cannot accumulate great power and authority.

5. Leaders of the power groups have an acrimonious spirit. Though they may make first impressions of kindness and gentleness, the mean streak emerges if you try to cross them.

6. A number of the members see those outside of the church as "them" or "those people." Therefore the church is at odds with many in the community instead of embracing them with the love of Christ.

7. Many members have an inward focus; they view the church as a place to get their own preferences and wants fulfilled. They are the opposite of the description

of church members in 1 Corinthians 12, where Paul describes them as functioning members for the greater good of the body of Christ. Many people in the community view these churches negatively. Those on the outside often refer to these churches as "fighting and firing churches." The community members detect no love for them from these churches.

8. Most of the members are silent when power plays and bad decisions take place. They don't want to stand up to the power. Their silence allows the power abuses to continue.

The Process and Challenge of Proving yourself in Leadership

Now the days of David drew near that he should die, and he charged Solomon his son, saying: "I go the way of all the earth; be strong, therefore, and prove yourself a man. And keep the charge of the LORD your God: to walk in His ways, to keep His statutes, His commandments, His judgments, and His testimonies, as it is written in the Law of Moses, that you may prosper in all that you do and wherever you turn (I Kings 2:1-3 NKJV)

This verse reveals a closing chapter in the life of a controversial and great king whose name was David. It was not only the closing chapter of a King but a aging father giving advice to his son Solomon. What does a father tell his son when he knows his season of life and leadership is near? David chooses to let his son Solomon know that his purpose now is to continue to leave a legacy of leadership. Notice he tells his son who was to succeed him in leadership in Israel "be strong and prove yourself a man". You will notice the verse says prove yourself a man. This could also be used to say, prove yourself a leader. The word prove derives itself from the idea of going through a challenging process in order that something greater of value may emerge.

I remember years ago, digital cameras, when a professional photographer took pictures with his single lens reflex camera he would take the negatives from the film and place it in a dark room and take it through a long process called developing. It was only in the dark room and the right small amount of light could he take what was a negative and turn it into something positive. His purpose was to get a clear image of something beautiful for others to see. David was telling his son in order to process or prove yourself a man you have to be strong and welcome the dark and difficult places that life brings. God will provide just enough light to get you through.

Psalm 23 tells us of the "valley of the shadows of death". The valleys were dark places but one doesn't have shadows unless there is some measure of light. Maybe this is why in Psalm 27 David tells us "the Lord is my light and my salvation whom shall I fear". Those dark places has a way of taking us into uncomfortable situations to reveal a clearer sense of God's vision and purposes for our life. God has a way of comforting the afflicted and afflicting the comfortable.

One of the realities of leadership is the challenges that often comes knocking on our door. When I lead Intentional Church Leadership workshops I often tell the attendees that in leadership you have to be intentional about your intentions. Many people and leaders in general unintentionally lead and are surprised at the unhealthy culture that has been created in their home, church and organization. The baptism of challenge always creates a clear and present danger for every leader. Let's briefly look in the New Testament Book of Acts to get a clue of the challenges a person faces as a leader.

The Acts 15 Model

In Acts 15, a serious conflict arose in the early church. God gave those leaders involved great wisdom in the midst of their present challenge. This is what I would call the Acts 15 model for redeeming church or organizational conflicts.

Challenge

And certain men came down from Judea and taught the brethren, "Unless you are circumcised according to the custom of Moses, you cannot be saved."(v1)

The beginning of conflict begins when one group intends to impose it's beliefs and ideology upon another group. There is usually low tolerance or a self righteous behavior and an inability to see the other groups point of view.

Perspectives

Therefore, when Paul and Barnabas had no small dissension and dispute with them, they determined that Paul and Barnabas and certain others of them should go up to Jerusalem, to the apostles and elders, about this question. So, being sent on their way by the church, they passed through Phoenicia and Samaria, describing the conversion of the Gentiles; and they caused great joy to all the brethren. And when they had come to Jerusalem, they were received by the church and the apostles and the elders; and they reported all things that God had done with them. But some of the sect of the Pharisees who believed rose up, saying, "It is necessary to circumcise them, and to command them to keep the law of Moses." (2-5 NKJV)

We can know for certain we have lost perspective if we begin to take conflicts as personal offenses. However, if we see so called opponents with eyes of compassion, we know God is working in us to redeem the conflict for his glory and our growth. Compassion is not just a feeling but should also place us on location where the challenge is so that we can see the situation from another point of view.

Leadership

Now the apostles and elders came together to consider this matter. And when there had been much dispute, Peter rose up and said to them: "Men and brethren, you know that a good while ago God chose among us, that by my mouth the Gentiles should hear the word of the gospel and believe. So God, who knows the heart, acknowledged them by giving them the Holy Spirit, just as He did to us, and made no distinction between us and them, purifying their hearts by faith. Now therefore, why do you test God by putting a yoke on the neck of the disciples which neither our fathers nor we were able to bear? But we believe that through the grace of the Lord Jesus Christ we shall be saved in the same manner as they." Then all the multitude kept silent and listened to Barnabas and Paul declaring how many miracles and wonders God had worked through them among the Gentiles. And after they had become silent, James answered, saying, "Men and brethren, listen to me: Simon has declared how God at the first visited the Gentiles to take out of them a people for His name. (V6-21)

If we embrace our personal and individual responsibility for leadership within each of our own personal spheres of interest and influence, we gradually become group problem solvers and increasingly turn away from narrow personal agendas. The more we see ourselves as shepherd leaders serving others among God's flock, the greater the opportunity for creating an environment from which peace and health will flow.

Biblical Response

And with this the words of the prophets agree, just as it is written: 'After this I will return and will rebuild the tabernacle of David, which has fallen down; I will rebuild its ruins, And I will set it up; So that the rest of mankind may seek the LORD, Even all the Gentiles who are called by My name, Says the LORD who does all these things.' "Known to God from eternity are all His works. Therefore I judge that we should not trouble those from among the Gentiles who are turning to God, but that we write to them to abstain from things polluted by idols, from sexual immorality, from things strangled, and from blood. For Moses has had throughout many generations those who preach him in every city, being read in the synagogues every Sabbath." (15:1-21 NKJV)

Notice he begins with "as it is written". We know that Christ loves his church more than we ever will, and that He paid more for it than we ever will. One of the biggest mistakes we make in the church conflict is failing to trust scripture. The word of God should be the point of agreement and resolution. Every conflict can be redeemed because the challenge of conflict can create resolution and be used for genuine spiritual growth.

Discernment, Consolation and Resolution

Then it pleased the apostles and elders, with the whole church, to send chosen men of their own company to Antioch with Paul and Barnabas, namely, Judas who was also named Barsabas, and Silas, leading men among the brethren. They wrote this letter by them: The apostles, the elders, and the brethren, To the brethren who are of the Gentiles in Antioch, Syria, and Cilicia: Greetings. Since we have heard that some who went out from us have troubled you with words, unsettling your souls, saying, " You must be circumcised and keep the law" —to whom we gave no such commandment— it seemed good to us, being assembled with one accord, to send chosen men to you with our beloved Barnabas and Paul, men who have risked their lives for the name of our Lord Jesus Christ. We have therefore sent Judas and Silas, who will also report the same things by word of mouth. For it seemed good to the Holy Spirit, and to us, to lay upon you no greater burden than these necessary things: that you abstain from things offered to idols, from blood, from things strangled, and from sexual immorality. If you keep yourselves from these, you will do well. Farewell. So when they were sent off, they came to Antioch; and when they had gathered the multitude together, they delivered the letter. When they had read it, they rejoiced over its encouragement. Now Judas and Silas, themselves being prophets also, exhorted and strengthened the brethren with many words. And after they had stayed there for a time, they were sent back with greetings from the brethren to the apostles. However, it seemed good to Silas to remain there. Paul and Barnabas also remained in Antioch, teaching and preaching the word of the Lord, with many others also. (22-29 NKJV)

So when they were sent off, they came to Antioch; and when they had gathered the multitude together, they delivered the letter. When they had read it, they rejoiced over its encouragement. Now Judas and Silas, themselves being prophets also, exhorted and strengthened the brethren with many words. And after they had stayed there for a time, they were sent back with greetings from the brethren to the apostles. However, it seemed good to Silas to remain there. Paul and Barnabas also remained in Antioch, teaching and preaching the word of the Lord, with many others also. (30-35 NKJV)

We see here that the letter is read, the people are encouraged. Judas and Silas gives leadership by strengthening the church with their presence and words. Judas is sent back with greetings from the brethren to the apostles. Paul,Silas and Barnabas remained to follow up and stabilize the situation in unity by teaching and preaching to the people of Antioch.

Conclusion

The challenge of a person in leadership is staying spiritually awake and being mentally conscious of the changing world around them. I am reminded of a story that Dr Martin Luther King often recited. It is the story by Washington Irving's Rip Van Winkle. The story goes that Rip Van Winkle traveled up to a small cabin in the mountains of upper state New York. Over his head was a picture of King George the Third of England. He went to sleep and woke up 20 years later and there was another picture over his head. It was a picture of George Washington the first president of the United States. The significant truth about this story is not that Rip Van Winkle slept for 20 years but rather he slept through a significant period in history. He slept through the American Revolution. While a great change was taking place in America he was not awake, he was asleep and he was not conscious of the new world and change around him.

A leader who desires to lead must never miss the precious opportunities to be aware of changing realities around them when the world is calling for their leadership.

CHAPTER 4

The Intentional Compassionate Leader

Connecting and empathetic to the people you serve

A critical aspect of a intentional compassionate leader is one who has a heart for the ministry and people that they serve. The essential idea of compassion is having empathy for another person. This leader is able, even at a distance, place themselves in the struggle,strains and sorrows of another person. They don't see those who work with them as mere pawns to further their personal agenda. The scripture below reveal the primary care an intentionally compassionate leader keenly aware of.

Be sure you know the condition of your flocks, give careful attention to your herds. Proverbs 27:23 (NIV)

When people know that they are not loved and not cared for, their motivation to serve becomes more of a task to be done or completed. This culture of caring has a way of translating and influencing, like dominoes to how the other persons within the ministry treat each other. In other words the leader over a period of time sets the emotional pace and grace of how the group will decide to intentionally treat each other. When we look at scriptures we see countless acts of the compassion of

Jesus to those he served. The bible tells us in Matthew 9:35 (NIV) an example of Jesus response to a certain group of people in their challenges and pain.

Jesus went through all the towns and villages, teaching in their synagogues, preaching the good news of the kingdom and healing every disease and sickness. When he saw the crowds, he had compassion on them, because they were harassed and helpless, like a sheep without a shepherd.

This scripture tells us Jesus was teaching and preaching and yes, even healing them of sickness. But when He actually saw them he noticed they were also a people who had personal struggles that were more than physical. You will note that he saw them harassed and helpless. There were emotional and oppressive situations that were daily challenges living under Roman rule and just the grind of living, even as they attended their church or worship setting. Jesus was sensitive to the life of a people even outside the walls of a church.

The compassionate leader know that those they serve are not robots or persons to be used to merely complete some assignment or task. These are people who need to be listened to and feel vested in the ministry. They need a physical touch for healing but also a touch of a arm around their shoulders letting them know that someone is there and cares for them. This type of leader knows that their words are critical to the health of those they serve. The right kind of word at the right time will reveal the heart of a compassionate leader. The book of proverbs reveals some hints about how this should be done. To be clear, this act of compassion is not only to sooth the heart but also to compassionately rebuke one another at the right redeeming time.

A word aptly spoken is like apples of gold in settings of silver. Like an earring of gold or an ornament of fine gold is a wise man's rebuke to a listening ear. Proverbs 25:11-12 (NIV)

An honest answer is like a kiss on the lips. Proverbs 24:26 (NIV)

A man of knowledge uses words with restraint, and a man of understanding is even tempered. Proverbs 17:24 (NIV)

This kind of leader has a way of restoring peace and calm in the midst of confusion. In fact a leader who is dispassionate, no matter how hard they try, doesn't achieve the results that they seek.

Proverbs 28.2 (NIV) tells us of a compelling truth

"When a country is rebellious, it has many rulers, but a man of understanding and knowledge maintains order. The ruler who oppresses is like a driving rain that leaves no crops."

When we look at the leadership of President Abraham Lincoln we see an instance of compassionate leadership in a story of one of his White House staff persons. His name was William H Johnson, a black man who was born around 1835. It is unknown where Mr Johnson was born. He began working for Abraham Lincoln, in early 1860.

The story tells us he took care of Lincoln's horse name "Old Bob", he perhaps swept the law office or brushed Lincoln's boots and coat, ran errands. Unlike the Irish girls, Kentucky men, Portuguese immigrants, and one or two other blacks who had worked for Lincoln, Johnson became personally close enough to them to stick. When Lincoln rode the train to Washington D.C. In February 1861, he rode with them, the only non official person to make this move. Conceivably there was a political or even social statement in Lincoln asking Johnson to join him in this journey to the presidency, but Lincoln's compassion and trust made this happen.

When Johnson, now finds himself working in the White House, is barred by lighter skinned staffers from his intended employment at the Executive Mansion because of his dark skin, had to find work elsewhere. Lincoln helped him get a clerk and messenger job at the treasury and Navy Depts. Johnson would still attend periodically Lincoln by trimming his beard, brush his coat, telling Lincoln what people around town were saying. When Lincoln prepared his famous speech, he wrote to the treasury to excuse Johnson from work, "William goes with me to Gettysburg." The story goes that both men contracted small pox in Gettysburg. Lincoln contracted a mild form known as "varioloid" recovering after several days. Johnson was not so fortunate. He contracted the serious kind and died in Washington D.C. in January 1864.

Johnson was without family or funds, faced a common grave, except that Lincoln paid for his burial at Arlington National Cemetery. A monument was placed on his grave reading "William H Johnson Citizen". This story revealed the compassion of a leader. Notice, that this kind of compassion embraced Johnson in a era of systematic slavery as not just an employee, or a black man but an American citizen to be honored and respected. We always see how a leader treats another person in private may well tell us far more than any public words or speeches he may have given.

When I think about compassionate leadership it forces me to look introspect fully in my own heart. When I look in my own life I see that there are lessons that my wonderful seminary didn't teach me about compassionate leadership. There are some realities I wished I had learned prior to my leadership as a pastoral leader. There are 3 key lessons.

1. Silence from your team does not mean they agree with you. Many times in the early stages of my ministry when I lead staff, board or volunteer meetings I would have a great ideas. So I thought. I would ask if there was any questions, and when none came I assume they agreed with my ideas. The team was reluctant to share their concerns. Only later would I find the idea was a not a good one and lacked support. My over bearing style and not being sensitive to their needs created a passive aggressive response from the team.

2. Compassion will get you further if you work together. If someone were to suggest an idea to me although I appear to listen, mentally I would often dismiss their idea if it didn't align itself with mine. Why? Because it didn't originate with me. Compassion would have told me to care enough to get their input and see others I work with with value.

3. Others in the group mirror the leader's emotional temperature. The term for mirroring another's response is call "emotional contagion." The team or group that we serve actually catch the emotional state of their leaders. Often times early in leadership I felt I had the right to get angry, pout or emotionally cut myself off from others if things didn't go well. I thought I was being authentic, or so I thought. Although the being authentic is important, I should have also brought a positive and

hopeful tone into the meeting. Negative emotions can and often create a dispassionate distance and lack of caring amongst the team.

Intentional Compassionate Leaders are Effective Leaders

Specifically, compassion have three components:

A cognitive component: "I understand you"
An affective component: "I feel for you"
A motivational component: "I want to help you"

The most compelling benefit of compassion in the context of work is that compassion creates highly effective leaders. To become a highly effective leader, you need to go through an important transformation. Bill George, the widely respected former CEO of Medtronic puts it most succinctly, calling it going from "I" to "We."

This shift is the transformation from "I" to "We." It is the most important process leaders go through in becoming authentic. How else can they unleash the power of their organizations unless they motivate people to reach their full potential? If our supporters are merely following our lead, then their efforts are limited to our vision and our direction. Only when leaders stop focusing on their personal ego needs are they able to develop intentionally other leaders.

The practice of compassion is about going from self to others. In a way, compassion is about going from "I" to "We." So if switching from "I" to "We" is the most important process of becoming an authentic leader, those who practice compassion will already know how and will have a head start. I looked the work of Jim Collins, documented in his book, Good to Great: Why Some Companies Make the Leap... and Others Don't, to be even more illuminating.

The premise of the book is itself fascinating: Collins and his team tried to discover what makes companies go from good to great by sifting through a massive amount of data. They started with the set of every company that has appeared on Fortune 500 from 1965 to 1995, and they identified companies that started out merely as "good" companies that then became "great" companies (defined as outperforming the general market by a factor of three or more) for an extended period of time (defined as fifteen years or more, to weed out the one- hit wonders and those that were merely lucky). They ended up with a set of eleven "good to great" companies and compared them to a set of "comparison companies" to determine what made the merely good companies become great.

The first and perhaps the most important finding in the book is the role of leadership. It takes a very special type of leader to bring a company from goodness to greatness. Collins calls them "Level 5" leaders. These are leaders who, in addition to being highly capable, also possess a paradoxical mix of two important and seemingly conflicting qualities: great ambition and personal humility. These leaders are highly ambitious, but the focus of their ambition is not themselves; instead, they are ambitious for the greater good. Because their attention is focused on the greater good, they feel no need to inflate their own egos. This leader makes them highly effective and inspiring.

While Collins's book convincingly demonstrates the importance of Level 5 leaders, it (understandably) does not prescribe a way to train them. I do not pretend to know how to train Level 5 leaders either, but I am convinced that compassion plays an essential role. If you look at the two distinguishing qualities of Level 5 leaders (ambition and personal humility) in the context of the three components of compassion (cognitive, affective, motivational), you may find that the cognitive and affective components of compassion (understanding people and empathizing with them) tone down the excessive self-obsession within us, and thereby create the conditions for humility. The motivational component of compassion, wanting to help people, creates ambition for greater good. In other words, the three components of compassion can be used to train the two distinguishing qualities of Level 5 leadership.

Compassion is a necessary (but maybe insufficient) condition for Level 5 leadership, and therefore, one way to begin training Level 5 leaders is compassion training. This is one compelling benefit of compassion at work.

Intentionally practice increased compassion in your relationships and ministry

The bible tells us compassion grows out of love. Let's look at 1 Corinthians 13

Love is patient, love is kind. It does not envy, it does not boast, it is not proud. It does not dishonor others, it is not self-seeking, it is not easily angered, it keeps no record of wrongs. Love does not delight in evil but rejoices with the truth. It always protects, always trusts, always hopes, always perseveres. Love never fails. But where there are prophecies, they will cease; where there are tongues, they will be stilled; where there is knowledge, it will pass away. For we know in part and we prophesy in part, but when completeness comes, what is in part disappears. When I was a child, I talked like a child, I thought like a child, I reasoned like a child. When I became a man, I put the ways of childhood behind me. (1 Corinthians 13:4-11 NIV)

When we look at the last verse of this portion of scripture;

When I became a man, I put the ways of childhood behind me. (1 Corinthians 13:11 NIV)

This could be translated…when I became mature and adult in my thinking I put immature behavior in its place. Compassionate thinking is mature and Godly behavior

Let's look briefly in application how we can move toward being more intentionally compassionate as a leader.

Stop thinking so much about yourself

This sounds harsh, I know, but there's an ancient Indian saying that the total amount of unhappiness in the world comes from thinking about ourselves and the total amount of happiness in the world comes from thinking about other people. It's the reason we get so excited, as adults, to give rather than receive. It's also the reason we want to see our children do better than we have, and why cultivating love and compassion for a partner feels so great in the first place.

Be aware

Emotions get carried away so quickly. Suddenly, any logical or reasonable alternative except for "they do not and will not ever understand me" or "this is another sign of how selfish they are" has no chance of winning out in our minds. Reflect on some of your past hostilities. Are there any hostile engagements or hasty conclusions you'd redo if you could? Use them to help you monitor the ways the mind can quickly jump from A to Z.

Pause

Once you have awareness of the lightning-fast way our minds turn molehills into mountains, use it. Some say our mood changes every minute-and-a-half. If the person in your group really hurt you or deserves to be called out on something, it can probably wait a minute. And in pausing, you're giving yourself the ability to check out your thoughts and evaluate whether or not they warrant the emotional response you've generated. Pausing allows you to double-check with your mind: "Do I really want to go in that direction? Am I sure there's not a better alternative here?" This can make all the difference in your business and in your ministry.

Do unto others

The golden rule: "do unto others as you'd have done unto you" has persisted in so many incarnations throughout time for a reason. If you are untruthful with your partner, don't you find yourself more paranoid that he/she's untruthful, too? Because you understand how it's done. Likewise, if you make a point of increasing affirmation or encouragement to your group, you'll most likely see a similar response returned to you. When you pause, keep this idea in mind. How would you want to be treated if you'd made a mistake like he/she had? How do you respond to someone shouting at you? And, how wonderfully unexpected is it to see others stop and try to see it your way (whether or not he actually succeeds! how great is the effort?).

Do your thing

While compassion depends on selflessness, if you are out of step, mentally, physically or emotionally, it's hard to see outside yourself. As a culture, we could be well-served to better honor respite, leisure and balance. The benefit of being fulfilled, of having worked out the kinks be that during a jog, a power nap, a yoga class, a course of graduate study or night away from the kids -- can't come from others. It can only come from you, and being a better, more complete and peaceful leader you will allow your relationship to follow.

Start now

Practice on everyone you know. That annoying coworker or at person at church? Think about what made him/her that way. What challenges do they face? Put yourself in their shoes and see if you don't feel more connected and empathetic to their plight. Say your wife is constantly "nagging" you to put your dishes in the dishwasher immediately after a meal. You don't see it as a big deal, but to her, it represents [fill in the blank] and at the end of the day, if putting dishes in dishwasher helps her to be happier and less stressed, why wouldn't you do it? When you feel you've made a misstep and acted without compassion? Start over. It's that simple. Be Intentional. Compassionate leadership creates a culture of health and care in any church, organization or group.

"Look into your own heart,discover what it is that gives you pain. And refuse under any circumstances, whatsoever, to inflict that pain on anybody else." Karen Armstrong

The Intentional Leader as a Compassionate Shepherd

The Lord is my shepherd (Intentional leader), I lack nothing. He makes me lie down in green pastures, he leads me beside quiet waters, he refreshes my soul. He guides me along the right paths for his name's sake. Even though I walk through the darkest valley, I will fear no evil, for you are with me; your rod and your staff, they comfort me. You prepare a table before me in the presence of my enemies. You anoint my head with oil; my cup overflows. Surely your goodness and love will follow me all the days of my life, and I will dwell in the house of the Lord forever. (Psalm 23:1-6 NIV)

The scriptures in psalms 23.4 speaks of God as a loving Shepherd leads his people through dangerous and difficult situations. But it speaks of the shepherd skillfully guiding and giving compassionate leadership with his rod and staff. The task of a intentional compassionate leader is to lead as a Shepherd Leader.

Notice the ultimate intentional leader we have in God; God provides 6 intentional behaviors;

He makes me, He is with us, His rod and staff comforts us, He prepares, He anoints, His goodness and mercy follows us.

The Leadership Tools of an Intentional Shepherd Leader

YOUR ROD AND STAFF COMFORTS ME v4

ROD

The rod was what the shepherd relied on to safeguard both himself and his flock in danger. And it was, furthermore, the instrument he used to discipline and correct any wayward sheep that insisted on wandering away. If the shepherd saw a sheep wandering away from its own, or approaching poisonous weeds, or getting too close to danger of one sort or another, the rod would go whistling through the air to send the wayward animal scurrying back to the bunch. Because of their long wool it is not always easy to detect disease, wounds, or defects in sheep.

For example, at a sheep show an inferior animal can be clipped and shaped and shown so as to appear a perfect specimen. But the skilled judge will take his rod and part the sheep's wool to determine the condition of the skin, the cleanliness of the fleece and the conformation of the body. In plain language, "One just does not pull the wool over his judge's eyes." In the same way a caring intentional leader is concerned about the condition and the life of the people they serve.

Also, In caring for his sheep, the good shepherd, was a careful manager, will from time to time make a careful examination of each individual sheep. As each animal comes out through the gate, it is stopped by the shepherd's outstretched rod. He opens the fleece with the rod; he runs his skillful hands over the body; he feels for any sign of trouble; he examines the sheep with care to see if all is well. This is a most searching process entailing every intimate detail. It is, too, a comfort to the sheep for only in this way can its hidden problems be laid bare before the shepherd.

Finally the shepherd's rod is an instrument of protection both for himself and his sheep when they are in danger. It is used both as a defense and a deterrent against anything that would attack. The skilled shepherd uses his rod to drive off predators like coyotes, wolves, cougars or stray dogs. Often it is used to beat the brush discouraging snakes and other creatures from disturbing the flock. In extreme causes, such as David recounted to Saul, the psalmist no doubt used his rod to attack the lion and the bear that came to raid his flocks. The intentional leader's pastoral care is similar to this process. This leader sends a level of protection and security to those they serve

STAFF

The staff is essentially a symbol of the concern and the compassion that a shepherd has for his sheep. No other single word can better describe its function on behalf of the flock than that it is for their "comfort." Whereas the rod conveys the concept of authority, of power, of discipline, of defense against danger, the word "staff" speaks of all that is long suffering and kind. The shepherd's staff is normally a long, slender stick, often with a crook or hook on one end. It is selected with care by the owner; it is shaped, smoothed, and cut to best suit his own personal use.

Somehow the staff is of special comfort to the shepherd himself. In the tough terrains and during the long weary watches with his sheep, he leans on it for support and strength. It becomes to him comfort and help as he performs his duties. There are three areas of sheep management in which the staff plays a most significant role.

The first of these lies in drawing sheep together into an intimate relationship. The shepherd will use his staff to gently lift a newborn lamb and bring it to its mother if they become parted. He does this because he does not wish to have the ewe reject her offspring if it bears the odor of his hands upon it. The staff is used by the shepherd to reach out and catch individual sheep, young or old, and draw them close to himself for intimate examination. The staff is very useful this way for the shy and timid sheep normally tend to keep at a distance from the shepherd.

Lastly the staff is also used for guiding sheep. Again shepherds use his staff to guide his sheep gently into a new path or through some gate or along dangerous, difficult routes. He does not use it actually to beat the sheep. Rather, the tip of the long slender stick is laid gently against the animal's side and the pressure applied guides the sheep in the way the owner wants it to go. Thus the sheep is reassured of its proper path.

Being stubborn creatures, sheep often get into the most difficult dilemmas. Many Shepherds had seen their sheep, greedy for one more mouthful of green grass, climb down steep cliffs where they slipped and fell into the sea. Only a long shepherd's staff could lift them out of the water back onto solid ground. The compassionate leader understands the caring and comforting role they play as a shepherd to those they serve. The reality and truth is, your people not only need to care about what the leader knows but also they need to know how much the leader as a compassionate shepherd cares about them.

CHAPTER 5

The Intentional Communicative Leader

Clarifying the vision, values and the
expectations of the mission

This person effectively shares values and the expectations of
the mission and organization. This type of leader understands
the necessity of clarity. They understand the boundaries of
relationships and that those who they serve in ministry are
unable to read their minds. This leader also knows that they
should not make assumptions that all those involved in the
group or organization understands the expectations before
them. This leader know it is not only what is *said* but rather
also what is *understood*.

This Intentional leader have a knack of seeking discernment
from God to figure out a way to create positive "group think". This
communicative leader understand "The Law of Navigation". In
other words they they have an internal GPS within them and
they know where they need to go in their vision and more
importantly how to engage the team to get there together.
They know essentially that a critical aspect of their legacy as
a leader will be that they are only as successful as they are
fully understood. Moses who led the greatest exodus in history
benefited from this.

So Moses the servant of the LORD died there in the land of Moab, according to the word of the LORD. And He buried him in a valley in the land of Moab, opposite Beth Peor; but no one knows his grave to this day. Moses was one hundred and twenty years old when he died. His eyes were not dim nor his natural vigor diminished. And the children of Israel wept for Moses in the plains of Moab thirty days. So the days of weeping and mourning for Moses ended. Now Joshua the son of Nun was full of the spirit of wisdom, for Moses had laid his hands on him; so the children of Israel heeded him, and did as the LORD had commanded Moses. But since then there has not arisen in Israel a prophet like Moses, whom the LORD knew face to face, in all the signs and wonders which the LORD sent him to do in the land of Egypt, before Pharaoh, before all his servants, and in all his land, and by all that mighty power and all the great terror which Moses performed in the sight of all Israel. (Deuteronomy 34:5-12 NKJV)

When we look at Moses and his leadership we see a man who first knew, as the bible states, the Lord face to face and he communicated God's purposes through signs and wonders. He understood that before he spoke to his people, he had to be spoken to and communicated by God. We see this in basically two instances. First, we saw this when God communicated and clarified His purposes to Moses through a burning bush to receive his mission to receive his calling to lead and to confront pharaoh. Secondly, God communicated to Moses on Mt Sinai his vision of what kind of people he wanted and how they should behave toward God and each other. Moses had to lead intentionally with the mission and vision that God had placed before him

A leader communicates to his team by word and deeds on a regular basis the mission and the vision. The mission reveals more of the purpose and priority that is before us and the vision reminds us of the dream and design that is in our common future. The reality is, this intentional leader through communicating these two realities are reminding the team that this work that we do is bigger and greater than any one of us but never greater than all of us.

Conversely, in the life of Moses we see a great man but he was also a man that God used in spite of his weaknesses. By his own admission, Moses lacked the ability to communicate well. *"I am slow of speech and tongue,"* (Ex. 4:10 NIV) was Moses' personal assessment. Most experts view the ability to communicate well as so vital to effective leadership, that it is hard to imagine how anyone could lead without this ability.

Even Geese Communicates

It's those intentional geese I find especially impressive. Winging their way to a warmer climate, they often cover thousands of miles before reaching their destination. Have you ever studied why they fly as they do? It is fascinating to read what has been discovered about their flight pattern as well as their in-flight habits. Four come to mind.

1. Those in front rotate their leadership. When one lead goose gets tired, it changes places with one in the wing of the V-formation and another flies point.
2. By flying as they do, the members of the flock create an upward air current for one another. Each flap of the wings literally creates an uplift for the bird immediately

following. One author states that by flying in a V-formation, the whole flock gets 71 percent greater flying range than if each goose flew on its own.

3. When one goose gets sick or wounded, two fall out of formation with it and follow it down to help and protect it. They stay with the struggler goose until it's able to fly again.

4. The geese in the rear of the formation are the ones who do the honking. I suppose it's their way of announcing that they're following and that all is well. For sure, the repeated honks encourage those in front to stay at it.

As I think about all this, one lesson stands out above all others: it is the natural instinct of geese to work together. Whether it's rotating, flapping, helping, or simply communicating by honking, the flock is in it together...which enables them to accomplish what they set out to do more effectively and efficiently. They reach their destination together because of how well they work together and communicated.

Communication as Motivation

Leaders can motivate or demotivate their people. They can propel them down a runway to great results, or confuse them so that they cannot clearly get from A to Z. They can bring a team or a group together to achieve shared, extraordinary goals, or they can cause division and fragmentation. They can create a culture that augments high performance, accountability, results, and thriving, or cause a culture to exist in which people become less than who they are or could be. And most of the time, these issues have little to do with the leader's business gifts or skill sets at all . . . but more to do with how they lead people and build cultures. Closely tied in with the skill of listening is the ability to express oneself in a nonabrasive and affirming manner. Listen to the scripture about reckless words and wise words.

"Reckless words pierce like a sword, but the tongue of the wise brings healing" (Proverbs 12:18 NIV).

We may teach our children to say, "Sticks and stones will break my bones, but words will never hurt me," but it's just not totally true. Words can hurt. Words can cut. In fact, at the root of the word sarcasm is the notion of cutting flesh. Anyone who has ever been on the receiving end of sarcastic speech knows the accuracy of that idea.

Once again, this is simply evidence of how much unbiblical pop psychology we have inhaled. The world would have us believe that since it's unhealthy to keep our emotions bottled up, we should allow ourselves to "vent." Unfortunately, this means we often use our words to vent anger, irritation, disappointment, impatience, stress, insecurity, guilt or whatever negative emotion we may be feeling at the time. Usually, those who are standing closest to us at the time are the ones who are wounded in the blast. Dietrich Bonhoeffer spoke of the need to practice "the ministry of holding one's tongue": "Often we combat our evil thoughts most effectively if we absolutely refuse to allow them to be expressed in words. It must be a decisive rule of every Christian fellowship that each individual is prohibited from saying much that occurs to him."

On the contrary, wise leaders think before they speak; in so doing they select words that nurture rather than destroy. When faced with hostility they speak gently, so as to subdue anger rather than stoke it. In his New Testament epistle, James tells us,

"My dear brothers, take note of this: Everyone should be quick to listen, slow to speak and slow to become angry, for man's anger does not bring about the righteous life that God desires" (James 1:19-20 NIV).

Those three commands (quick to listen, slow to speak and slow to anger) may be the most frequently disobeyed commands in the whole Bible. If observed regularly, however, they can radically change a person's life and help bring about the righteous life that God desires.

Your degree of ability to communicate will either evoke trust or distrust in those you lead. It will instill either confidence or fear. It will determine to a large extent how eagerly your followers will follow you.

The God Who Speaks

After he wrote the book "The God Who Is There", the great theologian and thought provoker Francis Schaeffer answer to that question is simple: The God who is both infinite and personal not only exists but he exists as a communicator. The foundational assumption of Scripture is not simply that God exists, but that he has communicated with us through the prophets and apostles, and most decisively through the personal revelation of his incarnate Son. As a personal and relational being, God is a communicator..... We are being 'spoken to' continuously.

Psalm 19:1-6 NIV contains a description of one way in which God has communicated with us: general revelation:

The heavens declare the glory of God; the skies proclaim the work of his hands. Day after day they pour forth speech; night after night they display knowledge. There is no speech or language where their voice is not heard. Their voice goes out into all the earth, their words to the ends of the world. In the heavens he has pitched a tent for the sun, which is like a bridegroom coming forth from his pavilion, like a champion rejoicing to run his course. It rises at one end of the heavens and makes its circuit to the other; nothing is hidden from its heat.

The first six verses of this wisdom psalm present God's general revelation to us through the power, order and beauty of nature. This revelation is general because it is available to all people. Without speech or language, the stars eloquently point beyond themselves to the One who created and sustains them.

Therefore no one is really ignorant of God's existence; his "invisible qualities – his eternal power and divine nature – have been clearly seen, being understood from what has been made, so that men are without excuse" (Romans 1:20 NIV).

The Tricky Tongue

Because we have been created in the likeness of God, we are personal, relational, communicating beings. The issue is not whether we will communicate, but how effective and appropriate our communication will be. Our speech can be a source of blessing or injury to others as James points out in his epistle. James is the wisdom book of the New Testament and like the book of Proverbs, James says a great deal about the words we speak. Chapter three underscores much of what we already know through long and painful experience: The tongue seems to be more difficult to bring under control than any other part of our being.

How do leaders develop and communicate a vision?

The first step is to understand what vision is, and the second step is to create a process for identifying and articulating a vision. Understanding this process will help you articulate your own vision and values, and will help you assist the leaders of your organization to do the same.

Developing and Intentionally Communicating a Vision

There is actually nothing mystical about vision. A vision is a picture of what an organization or ministry could and should be. A hallmark of great leaders is that their vision includes big ideas. Big ideas get people excited. Nobody wants to do something small. Leaders want to feel motivated about coming to work, because what they do matters. Some examples of big ideas that most of us are familiar with are Martin Luther King's "I Have a Dream" speech and President John F. Kennedy's vision for the space program, "We choose to go to the moon . . . not because it is easy, but because it is hard."

Great business leaders also know how to paint a vivid picture of the future. They make it look easy. However, most of them have worked hard to develop and articulate their powerful thoughts. The creative process of developing a visionary statement consists of four steps: Observe, Reflect, Write, and Speak. Here's what I tell leaders in my seminars about these processes:

Step One: Observe

In order to determine a vision, you must become an astute observer of your world. You have to immerse yourself in watching, listening, and wondering. Pay attention, ask questions, probe, discuss, and gather information.

Step Two: Reflect

Now you turn inward. For example, you look at important events in the church organization, or important events in your life and career, and ask yourself: What did I learn? What is this telling me? During reflection, you come up with stories and examples that form your vision and clarify your values. These stories enable you to speak authentically from your own wisdom and experience.

Personal stories are a rich source of material that can crystallize a vision. When searching for personal stories with leaders, we look at broad categories, both positive and negative, that usually yield some interesting images and help to communicate the vision and values that are important to those you serve. These include, among others: personal challenges, major changes, new experiences, lost opportunities, awkward situations, failed attempts, turnarounds, last-minute saves, inspiring people, remarkable achievements, and memorable events that may have occurred in their life.

Step Three: Write

Because we live in a fast-paced world, with little time for reflecting and writing, many people want to skip this step. That is a mistake. When you write, you discover how to say precisely what you mean. Many people ask why they can't just speak off the cuff. That is an important skill. But when you are articulating a vision, writing it down is a critical step in the process. The scriptures validates this in (Habakuk 2.2 NIV)

"Write the vision and make it plain upon tables that he may run that reads it"

A president of a college, was preparing to give his inaugural address. It had been "word-smithed" by an outstanding, talented speechwriter. But as he read the speech, people realized something was missing—himself! He had graduated from this school, worked on Wall Street,and served on the college's board of directors, who then drafted him for the job. But nowhere in the speech was there any information about why he accepted the position, what made him want to do this at this stage in his career, what his education at the college meant to him, and what his vision was for the college. He re wrote his speech and was able to identify two or three great stories that would tell people who he was and what he stood for. As he practiced the new speech, what came through and communicated was a leader and a person committed to the college's success.

Step Four: Speak

If you have followed the process, speaking and communicating your vision is a natural outcome. A leader is far more powerful and effective when he or she gets up to speak because of this process. Then, the speaking must be repeated. It does no good to create a vision without a plan to speak about it in many venues over a period of time. It takes several repetitions for most people to truly hear and remember the message.

Speaking well requires practice. All the preparation in the world will not wow an audience if the leader cannot speak fluently and confidently. There is no magic wand that will make a speech great if the speaker has not rehearsed so that he or she looks and sounds like a leader on the platform. The activities of observing, reflecting, writing, and practicing a speech are not usually on an executive's calendar, but they should be. A powerful vision, well-articulated, attracts people to an organization, motivates them to take action toward progress, and drives results. And you will be reminded that, as a leader, your language and your conversation will assist in creating the kind of intentional culture you desire.

Intentionally Communicating a healthy culture

To review again and it can said be said enough, the word of God speaks much about what we should say and how we should speak to each other. For example it tells us that speech properly stated is like "apples of gold". It tells us also that our speech needs to be seasoned with love. Let's look at some of the specific ways and samples a leader can use their speech and conversation to encourage, bless and sustain those God has blessed us to serve and lead.

Thank you
I'm excited that you are here

What would have been a better way to do that
What can I pray for you about
I am disappointed that you did that
I know you are doing the best that you can
How is your prayer life
What are any frustrations you are feeling right now
You are doing a great job
I appreciate you and all that you do
That's okay- you will do it better next time
I see God doing a wonderful work thru you
You bring wonderful gifts to our group
How Can I be more helpful to you
I know that must have been difficult for you
What do you sense God may be saying to you right now
How are things at home for you right now
Do you believe and think you have done all you could in that situation
I'm learning a lot watching God work thru you
I really believe with your gift you can do a better job
I really believe that this is not the right place of ministry for you right now

As you begin to live intentionally as a leader, practice communicating these words daily to the people you serve, your home or organization.

CHAPTER 6

The Intentional Conscious Leader

Being aware of the environment
around me and my limitations.

Intentional leaders are discerning leaders who have a conscious
and cognitive awareness of their ministry and organization.
They have a constant sense of what,where,when and how they
are giving leadership. This leader intentionally does a daily
personal self assessment and asking God "how am I doing?"
This leader is asking, Lord am I leading out of some personal
dysfunction or unresolved chaos from my past? Are their
persons within the ministry or group where I serve are being
limited in their gifts because of my limited vision? Have we
accomplished the goals and the mission we have established?
God am I personally pleasing in your sight?

We see in the life of David that God so moved in his life that
he was placed from an outsider as a shepherd boy to a insider
as king of all Israel. We see in the verses following that he was
aware and conscious of that reality, that all that he had and
accomplished came not from himself but rather from God. This
constant awareness I believe kept David in a state of humility
and thankfulness, even with his acknowledged human flaws.

In spite of it all God, in His grace, kept David in the position as leader and king.

Then King David went in and sat before the LORD; and he said: "Who am I, O Lord GOD? And what is my house, that You have brought me this far? And yet this was a small thing in Your sight, O Lord GOD; and You have also spoken of Your servant's house for a great while to come. Is this the manner of man, O Lord GOD? Now what more can David say to You? For You, Lord GOD, know Your servant. For Your word's sake, and according to Your own heart, You have done all these great things, to make Your servant know them. Therefore You are great, O Lord GOD. For there is none like You, nor is there any God besides You, according to all that we have heard with our ears. And who is like Your people, like Israel, the one nation on the earth whom God went to redeem for Himself as a people, to make for Himself a name—and to do for Yourself great and awesome deeds for Your land—before Your people whom You redeemed for Yourself from Egypt, the nations, and their gods? For You have made Your people Israel Your very own people forever; and You, LORD, have become their God. (II Samuel 7:18-24 NKJV)

Conscious You've Stopped Leading

Being in a leadership position is no guarantee we are leading. Holding the title of leader isn't an indication one actually leads. Leading, by definition, is an active term. It means we are taking people somewhere. And, even the best leaders have periods, even if ever so briefly—even if intentional—when they aren't necessarily leading anything. Obviously, those periods shouldn't be too long or the momentum eventually stalls, but leadership is an exhaustive process. It can be draining. Sometimes we need a break or a pause periodically for self assessment and rest.

For an example, I try to shut down at the end of every day and most Saturdays. I'm not leading anything—but I'm still a leader. And I periodically stop leading for a more extended period. During those times—I'm intentionally not leading anything. There are other times, such as after we've accomplished a major project, when I may intentionally "rest" from leading to catch my breath and rely on our current systems and structures to maintain us.

But, again, those times should be intentional and they shouldn't be too extended. In my experience, leaders get frustrated when they aren't leading for too long a period. For me personally, I like to evaluate my leadership over seasons rather than days. Typically, just for simplicity of calendar, I look at things on a quarterly basis and then on an annual basis. How and what am I going to lead this next quarter—next year? How/what did I lead last quarter—last year?

How do you evaluate if you are leading or simply maintaining? One way is to look for the results of leading. What happens when you do lead? And ask if those are occurring. Here are seven indicators that you're not leading anymore:

1. Nothing is being changed
   Leadership is about something new. Somewhere you haven't been. That's change. If nothing is changing—you can do that without a leader.

2. No paradigms are being challenged
   Many times, the best change is a change of mindset—
   the way we think. Leaders are constantly learning so
   they can challenge the thinking "inside the box."

3. You're not asking questions
   A leader only knows what he or she knows. Nothing
   more. And many times the leader is the last to know.
   A great part of leadership is about discovery. And you
   only get answers to questions you ask.

4. There are competing visions
   Leaders point people to a vision. Notice here I said a
   vision. Not many visions. One of the surest ways to
   derail progress is to have multiple visions. It divides
   energy and people. It confuses instead of bringing
   clarity. When we fail to lead, competing visions arise
   and confusion elevates.

5. No one is complaining
   You can't lead anything involving worthwhile change
   where everyone agrees. If no one is complaining,
   someone is settling for less than best.

6. People aren't being stretched
   There are never moments of confusion. Please understand. A leader should strive for clarity. But, when things
   are changing and challenging, there will always be times
   of confusion. That's when good leaders get even better
   at communicating, listening, vision casting, etc.

7. People being "happy" has become a goal
Everyone likes to be liked. Might we even say "popular."
In fact, some get into leadership for the notoriety. But
the end goal of leadership should be accomplishing
a vision—not making sure everyone loves the leader.
Progress hopefully makes most people happy, but when
the goal begins with happiness, in my experience, no
one is ever really made happy.

8. Conscious of Your Own Arrogance
I know at times that I can easily become full of myself.
This recognition of this truth keep me in check. The
bible tells us that "pride comes before destruction, and
an arrogant spirit before a fall" (Prov. 16:18, HCSB).
Use these potential markers of arrogance to avoid such
a fall.

The 10 markers you as a leader need to be conscious and careful in order to be not stuck on stupid

Marker #1: You believe few people are as smart as you are.

Not many people actually say these words, but honest leaders must admit they sometimes think this way. Some reveal this thinking by their ridicule of anybody else "not quite up to my level." Others assume they should be part of almost every discussion, regardless of the topic.

If you assume few people can teach you anything, that assumption should cause you to evaluate your heart.

Marker #2: Your first reaction to negative is to be defensive or to cast blame on others

If anything adverse (e.g., a lack of growth in the organization, a divided leadership team, a failed program) is always somebody else's fault, you might see yourself as above such declines.

In Jim Collins' words, you may join falling leaders who explain away negative data and "blame external factors for setbacks rather than accept responsibility."

Marker #3: Titles matter to you.

Check your signature line on your email. Look at your company's letterhead and website. Read the bio you send to others who have invited you to speak. Consider your reaction when someone introduces you without noting your title. Think about how you introduce yourself. If your title has become your first name, you've crossed the line.

Marker #4: You assume your organization cannot fail.

The bottom line for you is this: Your organization cannot fail because you don't fail. You are intelligent enough to figure out the solutions. Your track record is so filled with successes that failure is unimaginable. And, even if your organization struggles, you can simply replace your co-workers; after all, you are convinced that finding people who want to work for you will not be difficult.

Marker #5: Not knowing "insider information" bothers you.

Arrogance is characterized not only by a belief that we know almost everything, but also by a desire to know the "scoop" before others do. The most important people, we think, deserve to have the details first. If you get frustrated when you're not in the information's inner circle, you may well be dealing with arrogance.

Marker #6: You are disconnected from your team members.

Developing genuine relationships with employees is difficult as an organization grows. If, however, you see your team members more as cogs in a system than as valuable partners—or worse yet, if they perceive that you view them that way—you may be haughtily operating as "a steam engine attempting to pull the rest of the train without being attached to it.

Marker #7: Spiritual disciplines are secondary, if not nonexistent, in your life.

Disciplines like Bible study, prayer and fasting are more than simple Christian practices; they are obedient actions of persons who recognize their need for a strong relationship with God. If you are leading externally without spending time with God privately, you are leading in your own strength.

Marker #8: No one has permission to speak truth into your life.

Leaders who fall are often not accountable to anyone. Few of us are fully self-aware, and all of us deal with a heart that is "more deceitful than anything else" (Jer. 17:9 NIV).

Feedback is critical, particularly from those who can test whether we exhibit the fruit of the flesh or the fruit of the Spirit (Gal. 5:16-26 NIV). If no one plays this role in your life, your lack of accountability is likely evidence of pride.

Marker #9: Other people see you as arrogant.

Take a risk—ask others what they really think about you. Talk to the people who report to you. Interview those who formerly worked with you but then took other positions.

Be specific in asking, "Do I ever come across as arrogant?" Even the most emotional (and perhaps exaggerated) responses likely reveal some level of truth. Hear it.

Marker #10: This markers bothers you … or doesn't bother you.

If these words bother you, you may be coming face-to-face with reality in your life. If they don't bother you, you may be failing to see the arrogance that characterizes all of us.

Conscious in Discerning a Jezebel Spirit

I know your deeds, your love and faith, your service and perseverance, and that you are now doing more than you did at first. Nevertheless, I have this against you: You tolerate that woman Jezebel, who calls herself a prophet. By her teaching she misleads my servants into sexual immorality and the eating of food sacrificed to idols. I have given her time to repent of her immorality, but she is unwilling. (Revelation 2:19-21 NIV)

Let us take a deeper look at the character traits that goes along with the spirit of Jezebel". This spirit is much more than what meets the natural eye, and can be extremely difficult to discern for the untrained spiritual eye. There are certain characteristics that always seem to follow these women (and men) so you will be able to recognize them in your family, job, school, church, or anywhere else you go. You can only spot the Jezebel spirit when you understand their personality traits, so let's spend some intentional time under their skin.

Jezebel's character traits

1. The very first, and probably most outstanding quality of a person with a Jezebel Spirit, is their undeniable, ever-present need to always be right! In many ways these people are adult bullies. By the way again, this person could be a male or female, it doesn't make any difference. They are not humble people who seek the input of others, but have an unquenchable desire to "win" over you in everything. The worldly term for the spirit of Jezebel is 'malignant narcissism' for which there is no cure. Some traits of narcissism include: excessive self-love; firm conviction that he or she is better, smarter, or more talented than other people; becomes irritated when other people don't automatically do what he or she wants them to do; thinks most criticisms of him or her are motivated by jealousy; regards anything short of worship to be rejection; often complains of being mistreated or misunderstood; has fantasies of doing something great or being famous, and often expects to be treated as if these fantasies had already come true.

2. The second thing, highest on our list, is the "chameleon" Spirit"

They appears a certain way, but not actually be that way. They will adapt to their surroundings to seem like a loving, charming, and even peaceful person, all the while trying to get a hold of your soul. They will appear to blend in, and suddenly, out of nowhere, stick their tongue out, and swallow you up, by verbally attacking you. The Jezebel spirit is born out of witchcraft and is designed to destroy the host (which is the body it lives in), the spouse, children, family, relationships, marriages, the church, the prophets of God, and the body of Christ in general, in every crafty and subtle way possible.

3. The third aspect is their use of seduction, deception, and manipulation

The unwritten goal control is to your mind, your actions, and your destiny. She or he wants to see how far they can involve themselves into your life, and see how far you are willing to them allow to go.

Jezebel's usually come in two categories; the active, and the passive. Or as is has been said; the high-profile, and the low-profile. The high-profile, active Jezebel is the woman who is the leader of the home, including everyone in it. She is the one who "wears the pants" in the marriage/family, the overbearing, bossy, in-control, in charge, dominating woman, who is outspoken, bold, and militaristic. The low-profile, passive Jezebel is the woman who controls the husband and family "behind the scenes". She has a meek exterior, and no one would guess that she has the family in a head-lock, quietly controlling, manipulating, and destroying people's lives. She is soft-spoken, seeming submissive and nice on the outside, and only the closest family knows the truth about who she really is.

4. Jezebel hates children, especially her own - it takes great discernment to discover it.

The person with the Jezebel Spirit tend to treat their children cold and distant, rarely showing tears or emotion. They like to make sure they don't get any sympathy, because they hates weakness. They doesn't show much love or affection – genuine hugs, smiles, and affirmation are a rare gift. Usually, their children are merely treated as pawns in her game of control and achievement of power. They use conditional love to ensure their children's subordination. In this way, they will always strive for their attention and approval, and they will glory in it, only for their own self-gratification.

5. Jezebel will often mix religious terms and phrases to appear godly

The reality of this person is that their life doesn't produce godliness. Following a Jezebel 's life and example will lead to rebellion, darkness, anger, and strife. You will many times find a Jezebel person involved in various types of teaching activities; not only in religious settings, but also places such as schools and in various types of counseling. The reason for this is their need to be an influence to people. The spirit within them drives them to want to reproduce themselves and their teachings to other people. They like to be highly involved in people's personal lives, getting up close and intimate, making people confide in them. Then they becomes important, needed, and wanted, just the way they like it. Satan places them specifically in teaching positions so they will impart a distorted and untrue message to people, and thereby cause more spiritual and mental darkness to come upon their lives. People may be in a bad condition when they come to them, but they leave worse off than they came.

6. This person is a master of the "blaming game."

This person is extremely clever in gaining sympathy for themselves by producing convincing arguments for their case,

They usually portray themselves as fair in their assessments. They will twist and turn information to better fit them, even if it involves lying and crying, anything to make you be the responsible or guilty one.

7. Jezebel does not truly forgive people who offend them.

They keep track of all past offenses, and they use them to their advantage when they sees the need for manipulation. Their love is always conditional, making you know of the things that please them, so if you do not comply, they will reject you.

8. The Spirit of Jezebel often produces sexual imbalance and perversion in the children.

We have seen many examples of rebellion and extreme dark and obscure behavior in children and teenagers of mothers who possess the Jezebel Spirit. The family around them doesn't seem to understand why the children choose rebellion instead of becoming "normal" like everyone else, not knowing that it is actually not always a choice of conviction, but rather a direct influence by the distorting spirit of Jezebel operating in the family.

The control the children are under causes them not to develop as strong, individual, healthy human beings, but causes perversion and confusion, and sexual immorality. Children of Jezebel's can also fall in the exact opposite category, being overly well-behaved, submissive, pleasing, passive, and shy of conflict. They can be recognized by their fear, lack of ambition and self-esteem, many times rather wanting to take the blame for everything upon themselves, instead of searching for justice.

9. A Jezebel spirit will never admit any fault or wrong-doing.

If you plan to confront the Jezebel spirit with something, you can be totally clear about your problems, and your list of concerns, and yet come out on the other end, totally convinced that you were the only one at fault. The dark cloud of confusion that surrounds the Spirit of Jezebel makes you give up, and give in to their demands without proper reason. You don't even know what hit you, you just don't have the strength to fight them and you may even feel a sense of relief for achieving peace with them, not realizing the prize you are paying is compromising for the sake of peace.

10. The spirit of Jezebel brings about a tremendously powerful confusion that can make you doubt everything you stand for.

After your first few confrontations, you learn to stay away from coming even remotely close to suggesting correction. You find out, that you are not strong enough to stand up against it, and start becoming passive. This kind of passivity is what King Ahab suffered from, when he looked the other way, instead of confronting the wrong his wife, Queen Jezebel was doing:

When Jezebel heard the news, she said to Ahab, "You know the vineyard Naboth wouldn't sell you? Well, you can have it now! He's dead!" So Ahab immediately went down to the vineyard to claim it." (1Kings 21:15-16 NLT)

Because of King Ahab's passive negligence of Queen Jezebel's wicked actions, we have the term "Spirit of Ahab" which is the "perfect" counterpart to Jezebel. He wants to remain innocent, but is anything but innocent in the eyes of God. In fact the Bible says Ahab was an evil man, possessing the same persecuting spirit as his wife, as he mocked the prophet Elijah and called him intimidating names: "So it's you, is it — Israel's troublemaker?" Ahab asked when he saw him (Elijah). (1. Kings 18:17 NLT). Jezebel is calling Jehu names, mocking him and comparing him to another murderer: "When Jehu entered the gate of the palace, she (Jezebel) shouted at him, "Have you come in peace, you murderer? You are just like Zimri, who murdered his master!" (2. Kings 9:31 NLT)

Remember, Ahab's passivity cost him everything. The Bible says he sold himself to evil. In other words, it's not only through "old-fashion" Satan worship we can sell our souls, but also, when we sell our souls to worship another human being, who will drag us into a life away from God. No one else so completely sold himself to what was evil in the LORD's sight as did Ahab, for his wife, Jezebel, influenced him. (1Kings 21:25 NLT)

11. No peace around Jezebel

I believe, we have to understand, that dealing with the Jezebel spirit, will never be peaceful! One has to give, and that is certainly not going to be Jezebel if they have their way. A Jezebelite doesn't respect anyone, and certainly not someone of lesser authority than them. They will never humble herself and help find a way to make things work. Things have to be their way, or no way at all. King Jehu, the warrior, knew that there is no achieving peace, no compromise that can be made with Jezebel, only a violent counter-action can stop them:

"King Joram demanded, "Do you come in peace, Jehu?" Jehu replied, "How can there be peace as long as the idolatry and witchcraft of your mother, Jezebel, are all around us?" 2. Kings 9:22 NLT

12. In order to fight Jezebel you have to first come to their level of competition.

This means, you have to be as strong and fierce as they are. The Spirit of Jezebel is a very overwhelming and overbearing spirit that gives the Jezebel an arrogant and self confident flare and attitude, making them believe they are invincible.

They believe with all their might that they are the victim of every seemingly injustice committed against them up through their life, and they are fully convinced that anyone who doesn't buck to their authority, is against them, plotting their downfall. In many cases, the Jezebel has been the victim of sexual abuse in their childhood, and carries a huge grudge against the opposite sex or people in general. They demand "silk-glove" treatment. So, in order to combat them, you need to first be completely convinced in your belief about what you are dealing with.

How does one consciously deal with a Jezebel?

Every conscious leader after identifying the challenge before them is to not ignore this problem and just hope it goes away. It never does go away. You may have seen a picture of a man whose head is buried in the sand. He leaves his posterior exposed before others in order to exploit. In fact the potential for doing nothing is to let it fester and allow it to continue to cross emotional and spiritual boundaries until every thing that was developed is destroyed. When you are conscious of the "elephant in the room" it has to be dealt with and resolved quickly.

Suggested process for an intentionally conscious solution

Galations 6:1-2,7-8. This reveals what we should do
Isaiah 22:17-19. This reveals what God will do

Be in prayer in how to confront this spirit
Don't confront by yourself
Determine what is the end game of this confrontation
Be firm and be prepared for prolonged debate
Be prepared for this person to leave or removed out

1. Fight Jezebels with the power of prayer. The most common targets of church Jezebels are the leaders and church staff. I encourage everyone in vocational ministry to ask humbly for people to pray for them daily. One staff leader stated that in two of the churches where they served as staff, They had as many as 100 or more people committed to pray for them daily. They

typically prayed for him for only two or three minutes each day at noon. Their intercessory prayers were brief, but they were powerful and gave him wisdom.

2. Seek to have an Acts 6 group in the church. I am specifically referring to the manner in which the Jerusalem church dealt with murmuring and complaining. They appointed a group to take care of the widows who were being overlooked in the daily distribution of food. The seven who were appointed to the task were not only to do that important ministry, but they were also to preserve the unity of the church. Churches need to consider either informal or formal groups that see their ministry as dealing with conflict, complaints, and dissension so that unity is preserved.

3. Have a high expectation church. Higher expectation churches tend to be more unified, more Great Commission focused, more biblically defined, and more servant oriented. Stated simply, high expectation churches don't offer an environment conducive to Jezebels.

4. Encourage members to speak and stand up to church Jezebels. Jezebels thrives in a church where the majority remains in silent fear of church bullies. Jezebels tend to back down when confronted by strong people in the church. We just need more strong people in the church.

5. Make certain the polity of the church does not become a useful instrument to church Jezebels. Many churches have ambiguous structures and lines of accountability. Polity is weak and ill-defined. Jezebels take advantage of the ambiguity and interpret things according to their nefarious needs.

6. Be willing to exercise church discipline. Church discipline is a forgotten essential of many churches. Jezebels need to know there are consequences for their actions, and church discipline may be one of them.

7. Have a healthy process to put the best-qualified persons in positions of leadership in the church. Jezebels often are able to push around less qualified people who have found themselves in positions of leadership. There should be a spiritually and strategically designed process to choose and recruit people for key leadership positions.

8. Have a healthy process to hire church staff. For example, an egregious mistake would be the church's hiring of a senior staff member without the enthusiastic support of the leadership of a pastor. If the pastoral leadership and new staff member do not have good chemistry, a church Jezebel can quickly pit one against the other. A unified church staff is a major roadblock for a Jezebel spirit.

9. Encourage a celebratory environment in the church. Joyous churches deter Jezebels. They like somber and divided churches.

I hope these nine intentional suggestions can help keep or minimize the Jezebels in your church or organization.

CHAPTER 7

The Intentional Call of a Leader

Discerning that this is more than a job but
more about my purpose and mission

The real truth of a true leader is that they do not intentionally seek to be a leader. The call to be a leader intentionally seeks them. Often the challenges and the present needs of the times nurtures, ushers and calls this person into prominence and position.

For example we saw this in the life of a historic civil rights leader. His name was Dr Martin Luther King Jr. He had often stated that all he really desired to be, was a pastor of a local congregation. In fact his initial call was to be the pastor of Dexter Avenue Baptist Church in 1954 in Montgomery Alabama. The crisis of racial segregation in the city nurtured him reluctantly and often awkwardly into the calling of leadership.

This call initially isn't just a position with titles but rather more of a position and condition of the heart and spirit. We see an example of this biblically in the character of a young shepherd boy named David. He soon found himself ushered and nurtured into prominence because of the crisis of the moment that demanded his influence when others failed to confront

Goliath. The need of the times led him from insignificance to significance. The other reality is, as we saw with with Dr King and later with David, that this call is usually connected to a cause. We read in 1 Samuel 17 David responds to his brothers who questioned his motives and ability in confronting Goliath. David in a tone of frustration to them states "is there not a cause". The call is usually merged with a cause that drives the passion and demands our attention. It demands that we embrace it, penetrate it, transform it for greater individual and community redemption.

We also saw this redemptive call with Jonah who actually ran from God's calling upon his life and God intentionally allowed a whale to interrupt his rebellion and swallow him back to the place of need and purpose, which was Nineveh. God was calling him to transform a city. Lastly, we saw it in a young man named Joshua who was Moses assistant for years. God, as you may remember, prepared him along with Caleb to go and spy out the promise land and bring back a report. God moved him from preparation in being mentored by Moses to providing an opportunity to serve in a primary leadership role. We see in Joshua Chapter 1, that the circumstances of Moses death pulled him out of obscurity to opportunity.

After the death of Moses the servant of the LORD, it came to pass that the LORD spoke to Joshua the son of Nun, Moses' assistant, saying: "Moses My servant is dead. Now therefore, arise, go over this Jordan, you and all this people, to the land which I am giving to them—the children of Israel. Every place that the sole of your foot will tread upon I have given you, as I said to Moses. From the wilderness and this Lebanon as far as the great river, the River Euphrates, all the land of the Hittites, and to the Great Sea toward the going down of the sun, shall be your territory. No man shall be able to stand before you all the days of your life; as I was with Moses, so I will be with you. I will not leave you nor forsake you. Be strong and of good courage, for to this people you shall divide as an inheritance the land which I swore to their fathers to give them. Only be strong and very courageous, that you may observe to do according to all the law which Moses My servant commanded you; do not turn from it to the right hand or to the left, that you may prosper wherever you go. This Book of the Law shall not depart from your mouth, but you shall meditate in it day and night, that you may observe to do according to all that is written in it. For then you will make your way prosperous, and then you will have good success. (Joshua 1:1-8 NKJV)

I would imagine Joshua felt truly humbled and inadequate for the task ahead of him. He had to understand that he had to depend solely on the realities of the promises that God placed before him. Look at v 1-2 God gives Joshua a promise but also reminds him of the reality of the moment, "Moses is dead". In other words, it's your turn. The principle here is that there comes a time when one has to take a deep breath, release their fears, accept the moment that is before them and know this is their time in order to fulfill God's purposes for them.

We see later in this chapter Joshua 3: 5-8, the pronouncement of the responsibility of the calling. The principle here is that we have to examine ourselves, clean up to allow God to show up. The truth here is that God desires the leader to be a clean vessel.

But you are a chosen people, a royal priesthood, a holy nation, God's special possession, that you may declare the praises of him who called you out of darkness into his wonderful light.

Once you were not a people, but now you are the people of God; once you had not received mercy, but now you have received mercy. (1 Peter 2:9-10 NIV)

We see in Joshua chapter 1 God created space for him to give new fresh leadership to the Jewish people. God as a result gave Joshua the promise, pronouncement but also gave Joshua the power in Chapter 6:1-5 (NIV)

Now the gates of Jericho were securely barred because of the Israelites. No one went out and no one came in. Then the Lord said to Joshua, "See, I have delivered Jericho into your hands, along with its king and its fighting men. March around the city once with all the armed men. Do this for six days. Have seven priests carry trumpets of rams' horns in front of the ark. On the seventh day, march around the city seven times, with the priests blowing the trumpets. When you hear them sound a long blast on the trumpets, have the whole army give a loud shout; then the wall of the city will collapse and the army will go up, everyone straight in."

The truth here is that God may have us doing unusual and strange things in our calling in order for us to see His miraculous works and evidence of things we have never seen before in our lives. We saw three nuggets of truths in this portion of scripture.

Verse 1 We see an impossible situation for a leader. The city was shut up. The walls were 25 feet high and 20 feet wide.

Verse 2 We see the invitation to victory. God told Joshua in the calling "see I have delivered Jericho into your hands"

Verse 3 God gives the instructions for faith.

The intentional leader understands that their calling is not an isolated event or lone journey. They know it is a partnership with God shadowing them with wisdom for leadership.

The Greatest Leader

Jesus was the greatest leader who ever walked the earth. This is evident by the principles he taught as well as the number of followers that propagated since his day. Considering the influence he has had in history, he would be the world leader of the greatest spiritual movement in the history of mankind.

There is evidence to how he led recorded in the writings of Matthew, Mark, Luke, and John. These writings reflected his devotion to God, teaching about life and eternity, and the authority with which he spoke and acted. Leadership is influence; leadership is simple to understand in principle, and all one needs to know in leadership, whether good or bad, is to look behind them and see how many faithful followers support him. A friend of mine humorously once said that if you lead one step ahead you may have followers but if you lead too far ahead you maybe considered a target. In this case, Jesus has had more willing, loyal, and devoted followers than any man has ever had. Leadership is the ability to rally people together for one cause, and this is exactly what Jesus did.

Leadership Calling and the Intentional Principles of Jesus

Jesus is the ultimate intentional leader. During His life on earth, he turned three years of ministry into a worldwide movement that changed history. Today, more people follow Him than any other leader in the world. As a model leader, Jesus practiced, in his intentional calling, the most vital principles of leadership—and he provides an example for us to imitate. Here are some observations...

1. Leadership is servanthood.

"He who is greatest among you shall be your servant." (Matthew 23:11 NIV)

At the last supper, Jesus modeled servanthood by washing His disciples feet—including Judas Iscariot, the one who would betray Him! He showed us that servanthood begins with a secure leader (John 13:3 NIV). Jesus knew His position and was willing not to flaunt it. He knew His calling, and was willing to be faithful to it. He knew His future and was willing to submit to it. He had nothing to prove, nothing to lose and nothing to hide. He was into towels not titles.

2. Let your purpose prioritize your life.

"Father, I have glorified you on earth, having accomplished the purpose you have given Me to do" (John 17:4 NIV).

In many ways, the entire life and ministry of Jesus was about setting priorities and living by them. When He said, "Let the dead bury their own dead," Jesus spoke to the need to not be distracted from the real and most important goal, even those emergency situations that claim our attention (Matthew 8:22 NIV). When His friend Lazarus died, he stayed focused on what He was doing, and didn't leave to visit him for two days. He was a man on a mission (Luke 9:51 NIV). Leadership must be driven, not by the whims of people but by your God-given purpose.

3.   Live the life before you lead others.

"The good man out of the good treasure of his heart brings forth what is good, the evil man out of the evil treasure of his heart brings for what is evil" (Matthew 12:35 NIV) Jesus taught us to put "being" before "doing." At one point, John the Baptist sent a question to Jesus: "Are You the coming One, or do we look for another?"

Jesus could have answered indignantly. Instead, He said, "Go, and tell John the things you have seen and heard: that the blind see, the lame walk, the lepers are cleansed, the deaf hear and the gospel is preached to the poor (Luke 7:22)." Jesus let His actions speak for Him. He knew that people do what people see, not necessarily what they hear.

4.   Impact comes from relationships not positions.

Someone once told me that sometimes persons with titles feels like they have entitlements. It is amazing how pride enters into the heart of someone and they transform into someone that others care not to be around or even recognized. The scripture below gives us a clue.

"A new commandment I give to you, that you love one another, even as I have loved you, that you also love one another. By

this will all men know that you are my disciples, if you have love for one another." (John 13:34-35 NIV)

Jesus knew the importance of relationships. He did not set up a throne in the middle of each city and say, "This is my palace. This is the only place you can see Me." He went to the marketplace. He went to the boats of fishermen. He went to the synagogue. He went to the homes of people. He went everywhere. He "went through the towns, preaching the gospel and healing everywhere (Luke 9:6 NIV)."

5. Leaders must replenish themselves.

"Come yourselves out apart into a desert place, and rest a while." (Mark 6:31NIV)

Life is demanding. People are demanding. The more you succeed, the more you lead, and the more people will demand of you. Replenishing yourself in your calling requires your attention. Many times, Jesus would leave a crowd of people— the very people He was sent to serve—and depart into a place of solitude. He knew that times of solitude with His Father in heaven would enable Him to regain perspective and refuel Himself for what was to come. If Jesus needed to replenish Himself, how much more do we need to as well!

6. Great leaders call for great commitment.

"And He summoned the multitude with the disciples and said to them, 'If anyone wishes to come after Me, let him deny himself, take up His cross and follow Me. For whoever wishes to save His life shall lose it; but whoever loses his life for My sake and the gospel's shall save it (Mark 8:34-35 NIV)."

Jesus had the greatest product on earth: salvation. He offered the human race an opportunity to have a relationship with God. He spoke of heaven and angels, joy and peace, and mansions in glory. But, He never painted a distorted picture. He warned His disciples of persecution. He cautioned them about afflictions. (Matthew 24:9 NIV) He spoke of loneliness. (Matthew 8:20 NIV) Jesus continually prepared His followers for the tough times.

7.   Leaders show security and strength when handling tough issues.

"And He left them again, and went away and prayed a third time. Then, He came to the disciples, and said to them, 'Are you still sleeping and taking your rest? Behold, the hour is at hand and the Son of Man is being betrayed into the hands of sinners. Arise, let us be going; behold, the one who betrays Me is at hand! (Matthew 26:44-46 NIV)

Jesus handled tough issues in His calling, by intentionally

a.   Rising early and gaining perspective.
b.   Remaining calm during difficult times.
c.   Agreeing with His adversary quickly.
d.   Handling wrongdoing immediately.
e.   Finishing what He started.

8.   Great leaders lead on a higher level.

"In the world the Gentiles lord it over one another, but it shall not be so among you..." (Matthew 20:25 NIV)

Jesus led on a higher level than others, and called for a higher commitment from His followers. Jesus demonstrated leadership that was never satisfied with mediocrity. Leaders do not merely get by, and maintain what has already been. Jesus knew credibility comes from solving problems. His leadership surpassed normal expectations. Despite His own lowly beginnings, He led people to a life they could never achieve on their own.

9. Leaders choose and develop their key people.

"Jesus chose the twelve that they might be with Him and that He might send them out to preach." (Mark 3:14)

Effective leaders know their success is impacted by those who are closest to them. They do not leave this issue to chance. They select who will be on their team, and pay close attention to who will play crucial roles on that team. Jesus never took a vote; He made deliberate choices about everything, and even stayed up all night praying before He chose His disciples. He consistently challenged people to take deeper steps on commitment to the cause of the Kingdom. Principles of Jesus' plan of team building included selection, impartation, delegation, supervision and reproduction.

10. Intentional leaders know that there is no success without a successor.

"The works that I do, you shall do, and greater works, because I go to the Father." (John 14:12 NIV)

The 30 Dangers Confronting a Called Leader

Intentionally perceiving the realities around you
A wise man foresees evil. Proverbs 23.3 (NIV)

1. Trying to be all things to all people - trying to make everyone happy.
2. Not mentoring and inspiring new Joshua's in your ministry
3. Forgetting a basic truth; your people don't care as much about what you know-they want to know if you care.
4. Get caught up in micro management of your ministry
5. Forget that you will be subject to personal attacks on 4 levels; physical, lust, family and the leadership 3 C's Call, Competence and Character.
6. Have too loose of a management style without internal accountability.
7. Spending too much time alone with the opposite sex in your ministry.
8. Being emotionally distant from the people you serve
9. Not having clear expectations to those you are in ministry with.
10. Not determine before hand what "hills in your ministry you are willing to die on"
11. Thinking that you will not have a person in your ministry who will not be your personal thorn.
12. Not knowing the balance of when to manage your ministry and when to coach your people.
13. Public ally appearing to treat people in your group unequally.
14. Not spending enough time with your leaders
15. Running ahead of your blockers...out running Gods protection

16. Not realizing that you may see the bones but God sees the army
17. Forgetting to walk by faith and not by sight
18. Moving to quickly with you vision and ideas
19. Not recognizing your time to surrender to God things you can't control.
20. Comparing yourselves and ministry to what others are doing.
21. Taking the attacks and issues of the ministry personally
22. Not taking care of yourself - no balance in your personal life
23. Believe the work and group is totally depended on you
24. Not having any personal accountability and becoming a lone ranger
25. Having a inflated or deflated sense of self
26. Not sensing a need for personal continuing education to improve your leadership skills and gifts.
27. Not regularly being on your knees in prayer
28. Not realizing that people don't do what you expect … they do what you inspect.
29. Forgetting that you are building ministry for the next generation that should out live you.
30. Forgetting Gods call upon your life when things don't go according to plan

Be Careful of the Other Distractions to Your Call

I encounter so many struggling leaders. It may be through a blatant sin or a casual drifting from doing what they knew to be right, but it lands leaders in disaster. A pastor friend of mine said recently, "We need healthy churches and we need more healthy leaders." You need to remember that of the 250,000

Protestant churches in America 80% of them are in decline or in plateau. This is partly because there is not a clear intentional vision for creating healthy leaders. Research tells us over 4000 churches closes every year and over 1700 pastoral leaders are leaving churches monthly because of conflicts or burnout. The church in America, according to many recent studies, is in trouble and beyond the 30 dangers mentioned earlier there are a few more other leadership distractions.

1. Neglecting your soul. One of my mentors reminded me recently. "Don, don't forget to feed your own soul." It was subtle. Almost given as a sidebar to our discussion. But it was gold. One of the biggest dangers for a leader is when we begin to operate out of stored up knowledge of and experience with God. We need fresh encounters with truth and His glory.

2. Sacrificing family. Families learn to resent the ministry when it always trumps the family. Ministry families get accustomed to interruptions. They are part of the job as they are part of many vocations. But the family will hopefully be there when no one else is around. Ministry locations change but the family does not—so we must not neglect them. I've sat with people who lost the respect of their family. I know countless leaders whose adult children no longer want anything to do with the church. Apparently, there's not much that hurts any more than that.

3. Comparing ministries. There will always be a "bigger" ministry. Someone will always write a better tweet—or a better book—or a better blog post. When we begin to compare, it distracts us from the ministry we've been God-appointed to lead.

4. Finding affirmation among the rebels. This is the one that gets me in trouble among the rebels when I point it out to leaders. But we must be careful not to get distracted by people who would complain regardless of the decision we make. Yes, it stings the way some people talk to some leaders. And it's certainly not always godly how some people express themselves in the church. But what if Joshua had listened to the naysayers? What if Nehemiah had? What if Moses had given up every time the complainers were louder than the people who were willing to follow? OK, he probably was willing to give up a couple of times, but he held the course. If you are leading, there will always be someone that is not happy with the decisions you made. People bent on pleasing others—more even than pleasing God—have a very hard time finding peace and joy in ministry.

5. Poor boundaries. In an effort to "minister" to people, I know too many leaders who fell into a trap because they didn't have proper boundaries in place. The enemy enjoys a door of opportunity. Establish early your non negotiable personal boundaries in your ministry.

6. Abusing power. The leader holds a certain amount of power just because of their position. It has been said, "Unlimited power is apt to corrupt the minds of those who possess it." One of the more dangerous things I see, for example in churches doing these days is giving leaders too much power, without enough built-in personal accountability.

Conclusion

Remember the Titanic!

We all remember the story behind the Titanic. Many people may already know that the Titanic hit an iceberg at 11:40 p.m. on the night of April 14, 1912 and sunk just over two-and-a-half hours later. But many remember that while the ship was sinking the band begin playing in the midst of chaos. Sure, we don't want to create panic in an emergency but we also don't want to encourage complacency. Having the band play to give an illusion that there is no crisis is far from the most effective strategy for the orderliness in an evacuation to safety. Certainly, the captain or the leader should have an air of confidence, as mentioned earlier.

They must radiate the calm required rather than get into temporary face-saving tactics. Take action, gather the best people, ask for opinions, collect data and work out a recovery plan no matter how limited the detail. In an emergency, whether of the magnitude of Titanic or a ministry or a church that has collapsed, the best way to create energy is to follow the football strategy of getting in a huddle and call the next play.

Use All Your Resources

There is probably nothing worse than viewing the aftermath of a tragedy and knowing that there were options within arms reach that were never used. History records that the ship Carpathia arrived at the site of the sinking one and a half hour after the Titanic went under. Could they have used the engines while they functioned to come and lots of freshwater to hose in some flat surfaces? The bow anchors were not used and they certainly could have been snugged unto the berg to buy a few more precious minutes of buoyancy. Could they have assembled or collaborated the crew or a group of passengers to lash together several large rafts of wood furniture? this would also have kept them busy thus reducing the panic. Leaders in a crisis, must ensure that all resources are stewarded with great care. From time to talent to dollars, are you getting the most of all the resources available to you?

The Moral of the Story

None of us were alive when the Titanic sank, but all of us lost something that night. Hopefully, we can have compassion to recognize the lessons learned and will chart your course toward the right direction.Titanic was, by all measures, a disaster whose history we cannot change. We can, however, honor those who perished in the cold waters of the North Atlantic by learning the many lessons Titanic offers. It may never be from death that we save those we lead, but saving from financial, spiritual or emotional loss is just as important.

A true called leader understands these truths. They understand that it is not the icebergs that sinks our ministries or organizations but rather our lack of understanding and operating on the real truth about our reality. We need to understand that various icebergs will come our way. Think about it, much of the ice was beneath the surface than what was seen above the surface. The people we serve and the situations that are often before us are more than what we can visibly see. There are dangers and situations that are below the surface of their lives that are not seen that should allow us as leaders to pause with more caution before we proceed. We should but hope to create a healthier pathway for ministry and organizational safety. Again, it wasn't the icebergs that sank the ship but rather their inability to be conscious and navigate around them. As we understand these truths and also the icebergs beneath the surface in ourselves as leaders that we will position ourselves for more fruitful and dynamic leadership. Abraham Lincoln wrote about another critical way to navigate in leadership when we find ourselves with no clear answers or caught in the vortex of a difficult choice. Let me repeat this poem that was mentioned earlier.

"I have been driven many times upon my knees by the
overwhelming conviction that I had no where
else to go. My own wisdom and that
all about me, insufficient for the day"

Yes, this leader has to be intentionally on
their knees in intentional prayer.

Works Cited

Introduction

Proverbs 20.5 NIV
Deuteronomy 34.10-12 NIV

Chapter 1

Lincoln, Abraham, written by Lincoln to a friend after the second Battle of Manassas,to journalist Noah Brooks.
Pastoral Leader and Change, Article from Covenant Companion, June 2013 p.45
Jeremiah 3:15 NIV
Psalm 78:72 NIV
Romans 12:1-2 NIV
Psalms 63:1 NIV
Judges 6:11-12 NIV

Chapter 2

Gladwell, Malcolm,The Tipping Point, February 2000
Matthew 18:12NIV
Proverbs 11:14NIV
John 13:34 NIV
Romans 12:10 NIV
Romans 14:13 NIV

Chapter 3

Scazzero,Pete, The Emotionally Healthy Church, 8 Challenges
of a Leader, 2003
1 Peter 4:12 NIV
Nehemiah 4:1-6 NIV
Proverbs 15:31 NIV
Nehemiah 6:15-16 NIV
Ephesians 5:32 NIV
John 3:27 NIV
1 Corinthians 12:4 NIV
1 Kings 2:1-3NIV
Psalms 23 NIV
Psalm 27 NIV
1 Peter 4:12 NIV

Chapter 4

Abraham Lincoln Story, The William Johnson Story, January
14,1864, Chicago Tribune
Collins, Jim, From Good to Great, Why Some Companies
Make the Leap and Others Don't, October 16 2001, Harper
Collins
Karen Armstrong Quote
Matthew 9:35 NIV
Proverbs 25:11-12 NIV
Proverbs 24:26 NIV
Proverbs 17:24 NIV
Proverbs 28:2 NIV
1 Corinthians 13:4-11 NIV

Chapter 5

Schaffer,Francis, The God Who is There, interVarsity Press, 1968
Deuteronomy 34:5-12 NKJV
Exodus 4:10 NIV
Proverbs 12:18 NIV
James 1:19-20 NIV
Psalm 19:1-6 NIV
Romans 1:20 NIV
Habakkuk 2:2 NIV

Chapter 6

2 Samuel 7:18-24 NKJV
Proverbs 16:18 HCSB
Jeremiah 17:19 NIV
Galatians 5:16-26 NIV
Revelations 2:19-21 NIV
1 Kings 21:15-16 NIV
1 Kings 9:31 NIV
1 Kings 18:17 NIV
1 Kings 21:25 NIV
2 Kings 9:22 NIV
Galatians 6: 1-2,7-8 NIV
Isaiah 22:17-19 NIV

Chapter 7

Joshua 1:1-8 NKJV
1 Peter 2:9-10 NiV
Joshua 3:5-8 NIV
Joshua 6:1-5. NIV

Matthews 23:11 NIV
John 13:3 NIV
John 17:4 NIV
Matthews 8:22 NIV
Luke 9:51 NIV
Matthews 12:35 NIV
Luke 7:22 NIV
John 13:34-35 NIV
Luke 9:6 NIV
Mark 6:31 NIV
Mark 8:34-35 NIV
Matthews 24:9 NIV
Matthews 26:44-46 NIV
Matthews 20:25 NIV
Mark 3:14 NIV
John 14:12 NIV
Proverbs 23:3 NIV

ADDENDUM

Additional Resources for Intentional
Leadership Growth

Intentional Questions for Reflection

Now that you have read this book...let us examine ourselves.

1. When you read through the 7 Intentions, what three intentions would you believe to be your strengths

2. In the same way what do you believe from the 7 Intentions name 3 that you believe are areas of challenge for you now?

3. Place all 7 areas of Intentions in hierarchical order beginning with your strengths and end with your weakness as the lowest

4. What in this book would be a comment, idea, story etc that impacted you the most?

5. What is the greatest challenge you are facing in your leadership capacity right now?

6. Which character in the bible do you feel you are closest in character to right now? Why?

    A. Peter _____
    B. Paul _____
    C. David _____
    D. Moses _____

7. What have you learned about your leadership style that you didn't know 2 or 3 years ago? Write this in a paragraph.

8. Who are the leaders, whether in the secular world or Christian leadership that you align yourself in style to and why? List at least 3 leaders.
9. What are the intentional specific steps that you take to overcome your leadership challenges you mentioned in question 2? List the specific steps in sentence form.
10. What wise counsel would you now tell your younger self when you were initially starting off in leadership? State in a paragraph.

Leadership Behavioral Covenant

Talking to and not about or at each other as a group

Having "holy conversations" where you can speak the truth in love, and not have self centered conversations" where you beat-up on people who are not there and avoid speaking the truth to each other in love.

Behavioral Covenants—Holy Manners for a Faith Community: A behavioral covenant is a written document developed by leaders from Scripture, agreed to and owned by its creators, and practiced on a daily basis as a spiritual discipline. The Covenant answers the question, "How will we behave (how will we live together?) when we don't understand each other and when we don't agree?"

Behavioral Covenants in Congregations

Suggested Intentional Behavioral Covenant for Leaders
Colossians 3:12-17, 1 Thessalonians 5:12-26

I will seek to build each person up and not tear them down.
I will respect and honor the office of pastor, staff other lay leaders.
I will seek to communicate clearly and completely.
I will offer my opinions in love and humility.

I will make positive investments in each person life

I will seek to discover what is always in the best interest for our church or organization, not what may be best for me or for some small group.

I will accept disagreement, conflict and evaluation as normal and natural.

I will will regularly commit myself to prayer and care for the people I serve

I will strive to and seek to understand and not understood by the people I serve

I will not act as a boss but a steward and servant in the body of Christ

I will recognize the brokenness of the people I serve

Other _____

Finding Your Intentional Leadership Style

There are major differences in the ways gifted leaders lead their team. They all have the spiritual gift of leadership referred to in Romans 12.8, but they approached the challenges of leadership differently. I believe to be an effective intentional leader one must learn to manage the plan and manage the people. It is important to understand as a leader that there may be persons in your ministry or organization who may express one or more of these styles below. The management of these styles will create a shared leadership that could potentially create a more healthy, effective and efficient organizational and congregational life.

VISIONARY LEADER - these leaders have a crystal clear picture in their minds of what they want to happen. They cast visions powerfully and possess great enthusiasm to pursue the mission. _____

DIRECTIONAL LEADER - this style doesn't get much press, but it is exceedingly important. The directional leader has the uncanny, God given ability to choose the right path at that critical point where an organization starts asking hard questions; should we change or stay the course. _____

STRATEGIC LEADER - some leaders have the ability to break an exciting vision into achievable and smaller steps, so an organization can march intentionally toward the actualization of their mission. _____

MANAGING LEADER – some visionary leaders have a difficult time managing people. These persons take care of the minor day to day operation of the process. These persons take the big vision and break it down into smaller parts. _____

MOTIVATIONAL LEADER – these leaders posses insight into who needs a fresh challenge or additional training. They can sense who needs public recognition, an encouraging word to keep the positive fire going in a group. _____

SHEPHERDING LEADER – this man or woman love team members so deeply, nurtures them so gently, support them so consistently, listen to them patently and prays for them so diligently that the mission of the team gets achieved. _____

TEAM – BUILDING LEADER – team building leaders have insight into people. They find or develop leaders with the right abilities, character, and chemistry with other team members. _____

ENTREPRENEURIAL LEADER - these leaders possess vision, boundless energy and a risk taking spirit. Their distinguishing characteristic is they function best in a start up operation. They love being told it can't be done or that we don't have the resources to get it done. _____

RE ENGINEERING LEADER – some leaders thrive in a situation that has lost its vision or focus or one that has been staffed in the wrong way. This kind of leader loves getting a chance to revive broken and worn situations that have lost it way. _____

BRIDGE – BUILDING LEADER – this person is able to bring a variety of different people under a single umbrella of leadership so that a complex organization can achieve its mission. This requires a lot of flexibility. They have to compromise and negotiate and listen. _____

God has given all of us gifts and different roles in which each of us can be a tremendous blessing to our various ministries within the local church family. Many of us either has the biblical gift of leadership or is involved in the role of leader in various ways. Hopefully this will assist you in developing a healthy understanding how you can contribute to your work.

Intentional Assignment

1. Check off one to three areas that you believe closely align with your leadership style or/and you can have someone else who knows you to give their opinion. Place in order of your strengths.
2. Discuss your choice, how their leadership style would be necessary in certain situations. Create and give examples.
3. If you are in a group, let this be a group assessment time. Have each person to share their primary, secondary and tertiary leadership style. Talk to each other about how each adds value to your team's mission.

Case Studies for Intentional Discussion

1. You are very excited on being the new leader in you ministry. You have worked hard on getting prepared for your first meeting. You have the agenda, the mission statement, your vision statement,goals as well as suggested activities. You are ready for Input from the other members of your ministry. There is only One problem....only a few people show up for the meeting...

2. In exactly one month the ministry in the church in which you lead will be having its first major fund raiser. The committees were assigned months ago. At the meeting, the agenda now calls for committee reports. Much to your surprise, no one is ready - where do you go from here?

3. Several members of your ministry come to you in love and tell you they along with other members, feel like you are a dictator and you want everything to go your way and they have no input. It is even to the point where they want to resign. They voice their concerns to you and other you suggestions. How do you respond to them and where do you go from here?

Instructions

Break into small groups for 30 minutes to discuss and present your findings to the whole group

"Hope has two beautiful daughters: their names are anger and courage. Anger that things are the way they are. Courage to make them the way they ought to be." St. Augustine

The Intentional Leader Role: Understanding your people thru their unique personality

The DISC Method (Dominance, Influencing, Steadiness and Compliance)

"I know my sheep and my sheep knows me" John 10:14 NIV

Intentional Leadership in counseling/ conflicts thru understanding their DISC

Ezekiel 34:1-10 "The word of the Lord came unto me. Son of man prophesy against the shepherds of Israel; prophesy and say unto them; this is what the Sovereign Lord says, woe to the shepherds (leaders)of Israel who only take care of themselves, should not the shepherds (leaders) take care of the flock.

Communication

2 Timothy 2:15 NIV Present yourself approved a workman not ashamed rightly handling the word of truth

D   Be honest and clear. To get their attention be direct and to the point. They appreciate the word of God Challenging them to live a Godly life. Sell them the idea of the rewards and consequences of what they will do in ministry. This type of a member thrives on a challenge. The bible tells us that the Apostle Paul was a high D. Acts 9 3-6 NIV

I   Be excited. This person needs the leader to give clear directions in their presentation. These persons desire a word that is positive and inspirational. To capture their attention show them alternatives to the truths and principles that you will preach or teach. This person thrives on opportunities that are placed before them.

Peter was a High I. Matthew 26:31-35,69-75 NIV

S   This person thrives on encouragement when the preach word is presented. This person loves to hear about process more than the product itself. They like to hear about relationships and harmony.

The bible tells us of a man name Abraham who was a High S. Genesis 16:1-6 NIV

C   Be specific and accurate in your information. To capture their attention your presentation needs to be factual. It is important that you prepare your sermons in a way that shows the pew that you have done your home work.

The Old Testament tells of a man name Moses who was a High C, Exodus 19, Exodus 3:1-22 NIV

Counseling and Conflicts

1Thessalonians 5:14NIV "we urge you to warn those who are idle, encourage, help the weak, be patient with everyone."

D This person wants you to be straight and to the point. They want to know what is on your mind. Focus on actions and how to achieve the goal. Caring confrontation may be necessary to get their attention.

Solomon was a high D Solomon 9:1-9. NIV

I This person is a affiliator, negotiator, persuader and encourager. This person responds to clear instructions. Sometimes this person has a tendency to shift blame. Confrontation in the form of questions that ask them to explain their actions.

Aaron and David were a High I. Exodus 32:21-24 NIV

S This person responds in counseling and conflict when they are sense that they are understood and are accepted for who they are. When they sense that you care, the leader can get more mileage from them. Usually before they are confronted encouragement first helps them to fully receive your information. These persons are steady and consistent. They have a tendency to be very industrious and diligent people.

Martha was a High S Luke 10:38-42 NIV

C This person has a tendency to be critical of self. They desire to know specifically what can I do to improve and grow into a better person. They prefer a inch by inch slow approach to change. When sudden decisions are made for quick changes this can be a very difficult situation for them to adjust to. Answer their questions in a patient and persistent manner. Thomas and Luke were High C. Luke 1:1-4,Acts 1:1-2 NIV

Task and Assignment

If you are in a group,organization or ministry list the names of the people you serve with. Place by each name,even with your limited knowledge of personalities, which one of the above DISC personalities that you believe at this time correlates with them. For more information on DISC personalities check and research the many resources and books concerning this.

Printed in the United States
By Bookmasters